Nature's Own
VEGETABLE
COOKBOOK

Nature's Own VEGETABLE COOKBOOK

by Ann Williams-Heller

AN ARC BOOK

ARCO PUBLISHING COMPANY, INC.
219 Park Avenue South, New York, N.Y. 10003

TO MOTHER

"I have given you every herb bearing seed, which
is upon the face of the earth, and every tree,
in which is the fruit of a tree yielding seed; to
you it shall be for meat."—*Genesis* 1:29

An ARC Book
Published by Arco Publishing Company, Inc.
219 Park Avenue South, New York, N.Y. 10003

Copyright © 1945, 1973 by Ann Williams-Heller

ISBN 0-668-02586-7

Printed in the United States of America

Contents

Foreword   v
Back to Nature . . !   vii

Part One: What It's All About
  Nutrition Facts for Food Selection   3
  Vegetables from Store to Stove   15
  The Salad Bowl   18
  Kitchen Shortcuts, Pots and Pans   23

Part Three: What and How — In a Nutshell
  The Daily Menus Planner   31
  Vegetable Groups in the Daily
    Menu Planner   32
  Buying Guide for Fresh Vegetables   35
  Cleaning Guide   49
  Storage Guide   50
  Cooking Guide   54
    Fresh Vegetables   60
    Dried Vegetables (Legumes)   73
    Canned   Vegetables   74
    Frozen Vegetables   74
  Seasoning Guide   75

Part Three: Recipes "Cooked to Your Taste"
  Introduction   79
  Fresh Vegetables   82
  Legumes   165
  Soups   169
  Salads   178
  Sauces and Salad Dressings   192

Index   202

Foreword

FRESH VEGETABLES are Mother Nature's bountiful and precious gift to mankind. She put all her love and imagination, indeed all her beauty and wealth into a never-ending variety of "fruits from the soil." Fresh vegetables are filled with color and flavor to delight and satisfy man's senses and make him live healthfully.

If this sounds like a fairy tale of old, it is not said lightly. For the fruits of the soil—second to no other group of our foods—provide an overwhelming abundance of minerals and vitamins that are easily assimilated, and help maintain the body's alkaline balance. Not all vegetables are alike, of course. Some are rich in body-building proteins; others supply carbohydrates and fats for energy. All vegetables carry bulk (cellulose) and water, both of which are necessary to "sweep" our system clean.

Vegetables—the edible portions of plants—are all eaten in their natural state, whether they be (1) the *leaves* of cabbage, chicory, dandelions, endive, lettuce, spinach or watercress; (2) the *roots, bulbs or tubers* of beets, carrots, celeriac (knob celery), Jerusalem artichokes, kohlrabi, onions, potatoes and yams, radishes or turnips; (3) the *stems* of celery, leek or green onions; (4) the *sprouts* or tender shoots of asparagus; (5) the *flowering heads* of cauliflower or globe artichokes; (6) the *fruits* of cucumbers, peppers, pumpkins, squash or tomatoes; (7) the *seeds* (before or after full ripeness) of corn on the cob, lima beans, green peas and all legumes, or (8) the *fungi* of fast-growing mushrooms.

Those concerned with overweight can happily increase their daily meals' quantity and variety by including up to two servings (one-half to one cup each) of these *low-calorie vegetables:* asparagus, snap beans, beet greens, broccoli, cabbage, cauliflower, celery, chard, chicory, collard greens, cucumbers, dandelion greens, endive, escarole, kale, all lettuce varieties, mung bean sprouts, mushrooms, mustard greens, green peppers, radishes, spinach, sauerkraut, summer squash, tomatoes, turnip greens and watercress.

Unfortunately, fresh vegetables are so often boiled to death, stripped and robbed of their vivid color, crisp texture and flavor, and—alas—also of their nutritional wealth. However, with the proper know-how, vegetables can easily be served in an infinite variety of appetizing main dishes, casseroles, full-meal salads, soups and unusual side dishes. And this is what this book is all about—from Artichokes Italian style to Zucchini Provencale.

May the 350 recipes in this book add as much to your meal enjoyment as they will contribute to your health protection. For with fresh vegetables, good food and sound nutrition are one and the same!

ANN WILLIAMS-HELLER

Back To Nature . . . !

WITH THE RAPIDLY increasing interest in food ecology, "organically grown foods" seem to fill a need of the time. More homemakers are looking for what one expert recently described as "foods produced on remineralized soils, rich in humus and biologically composted natural fertilizers without the use of synthetic agricultural chemicals, dusts and sprays."

Today, all those concerned with organically grown vegetables will find them in a selective variety in numerous health-food stores in larger cities. For nearby stores, consult the yellow pages of the telephone directory. Elsewhere, some will grow their own garden-fresh vegetables organically or look for nearby farms that grow them.

Vegetarians as well as "back to nature" followers who wish to serve *"pure and whole foods"* can easily use the recipes in this book by consulting the following list of eighteen common foods. The "pure foods" contain no preservatives, additives, artificial flavors and colors, emulsifiers, chemicals and stabilizers. "Whole" flour and cereal products are not highly refined, but left whole before processing and manufacturing.

If these natural "health foods" are not on shelf in regular supermarkets, they are available in health-food stores.

FOODS USED IN THE RECIPES OF THIS BOOK
(In Alphabetical Order)

Regular	Natural or Organic
Bouillon cubes	Vegetable cubes or powder
Breads, cubed or crumbs	Whole-grain
Butter	Natural butter or vegetable butter (almond, cashew, peanut or sesame) or oil
Canned foods	Check labels; with no additives, chemicals or stabilizers added
Cheese	Natural
Cornstarch	Arrowroot
Flour	Natural, unbleached, whole-grain, stone-ground
Frozen foods	Same as canned foods
Gelatine	Agar-agar flakes
Milk or cream	Soybean milk (fresh or powder), soy cream
Oil	Cold-pressed; according to flavor preference
Prunes	Unsulfured
Raisins	Unsulfured
Rice	Natural, brown
Salt	According to preference: vegetized (vegetable) salts, sea salt, powdered sea weed (Kelp); sodium-free salt substitutes
Sugar	Brown sugar, organic honey
Fresh Vegetables	Organically grown
Vinegar	Natural; according to flavor preference

PART ONE

What It's All About

Nutrition Facts For Food Selection

WHILE THE JOY of good eating is vital to our physical and mental well-being, food satisfies a *basic need* of every man, woman and child...a need second only to that of the air they breathe. Since this need for food is life-essential and constantly recurring, we must eat regularly. To be truly health-protecting, meals must balance nutritionally. Among all food groups, it is the color-full and flavor-full fresh vegetables that are first in line for such constructive health protection.

Today, the science of nutrition is part and parcel of preventive and corrective medicine. To keep the complicated human body machine in good working order, an impressively numerous variety of "food elements" is required; so important are they that scientists call them "dietary essentials." Within the human body, each essential food element makes its definite contribution for which no other can substitute. Therefore, an *over*supply of any one food element can not pinch-hit for an *under*supply of another. With our daily meals it is the "altogether" . . . the proper balance that counts!

All food elements, as they travel into man's body with his meals, work as a team . . . silently and unwatched by the human eye. As links in an invisible chain, all the many food elements are equally important to man's health, although not all are needed in equal quantities or in the same amounts for each human being.

Individual needs vary with age, sex, height, the rate at which the body works (basal metabolic rate), physical activity (occupation as well as exercise), and also climate. The individual daily dietary requirements of various food elements as recommended by the Food and Nutritition Board, National Research Council (in its publication 1694 [1968] of the National Academy of Sciences, Washington, D.C., 20418) are listed in Chart 1.

Today's modern homemaker is fully aware what the science of nutrition has to offer. Nutritionally balanced meals mean protective eating. Therefore, nutrition becomes a simple four-letter word: F-o-o-d. If meals were unbalanced for a longer period of time, it would show in the body's decreased vitality and resistance before actual deficiency diseases manifest. Therefore, the modern homemaker—in her planning, marketing, cooking and serving attractive meals—wants to keep the following facts in mind.

To run the body smoothly, foods must supply:

1) *Energy* (or fuel)which is measured in *calories*. Main sources are carbohydrates (sugars and starches) and fats. Bread, cereals and starchy vegetables supply the starches, while sugars come in the form of sugar and honey; also with fruit, milk and some vegetables. Of fats (the most concentrated form of energy), there are vegetable oils, butter and animal fats.

2) *Proteins,* the chemical base of all human cells, are chiefly responsible for the rebuilding of worn-out tissues and the making of new. Rich sources of good proteins are milk, eggs and cheese; all meats and sea foods; soybeans, dried beans, lentils and peas, and peanuts and nuts of vegetable origin.

3) Tiny yet mighty *minerals* maintain the balance of body fluids and regulate the proper functioning of all tissues. Some minerals, such as calcium, iron and phosphorus, do also participate in the actual building of body cells.

4) Even tinier *vitamins,* often called "giant spark plugs," help kindle and regulate bodily processes and hormone activity. Some vitamins supply body-building material, others are vital to the complete utilization of foods consumed. Since most vitamins cannot be stored in the body, their adequate daily supply must come from food; a lack causes deficiency diseases in the long run.

5) *Roughage,* also known as bulk or cellulose in foods, acts as an efficient broom in eliminating waste products.

While minerals, vitamins and roughage—in themselves—do not carry any fuel value (calories), their presence is needed to make the energy (calories) inherent in foods fully available and utilized. Vegetables again are first in line on all three counts, as they are indeed also in many other body-regulating activities.

For a detailed illustration, see the Nutritional Menu Planning Guide in Chart 2, and also consult Food Elements—What They Are and What They Do—in Chart 3.

Easy-to-follow charts in Part Two of this book present important facts to guide every conscientious homemaker step by step in simple "how-to" fashion—illustrating how to plan meals with ease and nutritional security, shop economically, care for vegetables in the home, cook and season them tastefully.

Charts

1. Recommended Daily Dietary Allowances
   (as recommended by the Food and
   Nutrition Board, National Research Council)   8–9

2. Nutritional Menu Planning Guide   10–11

3. Food Elements—What They Do and Where
   They Are   12

The Daily Menu Planner   31
Vegetable Groups in the Daily
Menu Planner   32–34
Foods Used in the Recipes of This Book   x

CHART 1

RECOMMENDED DIETARY ALLOWANCES*
Food and Nutrition Board, National Research Council

	Age (years) From Up to	Weight (kg)	Weight (lbs)	Height cm	Height (in.)	kcal	Protein (gm)	Vitamin A Activity (IU)	Vitamin D (IU)	Vitamin E Activity (IU)
Infants	0 - 1/6	4	9	55	22	kg × 120	kg × 2.2	1,500	400	5
	1/6 - 1/2	7	15	63	25	kg × 110	kg × 2.0	1,500	400	5
	1/2 - 1	9	20	72	28	kg × 100	kg × 1.8	1,500	400	5
Children	1 - 2	12	26	81	32	1,100	25	2,000	400	10
	2 - 3	14	31	91	36	1,250	25	2,000	400	10
	3 - 4	16	35	100	39	1,400	30	2,500	400	10
	4 - 6	19	42	110	43	1,600	30	2,500	400	10
	6 - 8	23	51	121	48	2,000	35	3,500	400	15
	8 - 10	28	62	131	52	2,200	40	3,500	400	15
Males	10 - 12	35	77	140	55	2,500	45	4,500	400	20
	12 - 14	43	95	151	59	2,700	50	5,000	400	20
	14 - 18	59	130	170	67	3,000	60	5,000	400	25
	18 - 22	67	147	175	69	2,800	60	5,000	400	30
	22 - 35	70	154	175	69	2,800	65	5,000	—	30
	35 - 55	70	154	173	68	2,600	65	5,000	—	30
	55 - 75+	70	154	171	67	2,400	65	5,000	—	30
Females	10 - 12	35	77	142	56	2,250	50	4,500	400	20
	12 - 14	44	97	154	61	2,300	50	5,000	400	20
	14 - 16	52	114	157	62	2,400	55	5,000	400	25
	16 - 18	54	119	160	63	2,300	55	5,000	400	25
	18 - 22	58	128	163	64	2,000	55	5,000	400	25
	22 - 35	58	128	163	64	2,000	55	5,000	—	25
	35 - 55	58	128	160	63	1,850	55	5,000	—	25
	55 - 75+	58	128	157	62	1,700	55	5,000	—	25
Pregnancy						+200	65	6,000	400	30
Lactation						+1,000	75	8,000	400	30

*The allowance levels are intended to cover individual variations among most normal persons as they live in the United States under usual environmental stresses. The recommended allowances can be attained with a variety of common foods, providing other nutrients for which human requirements have been less well defined.

CHART 1 *Continued*

RECOMMENDED DIETARY ALLOWANCES*

Food and Nutrition Board, National Research Council

Water-Soluble Vitamins							Minerals				
Ascorbic Acid (mg)	Folacin (mg)	Niacin (mg equiv)	Riboflavin (mg)	Thiamin (mg)	Vitamin B_6 (mg)	Vitamin B_{12} (µg)	Calcium (g)	Phosphorus (g)	Iodine (µg)	Iron (mg)	Magnesium (mg)
35	0.05	5	0.4	0.2	0.2	1.0	0.4	0.2	25	6	40
35	0.05	7	0.5	0.4	0.3	1.5	0.5	0.4	40	10	60
35	0.1	8	0.6	0.5	0.4	2.0	0.6	0.5	45	15	70
40	0.1	8	0.6	0.6	0.5	2.0	0.7	0.7	55	15	100
40	0.2	8	0.7	0.6	0.6	2.5	0.8	0.8	60	15	150
40	0.2	9	0.8	0.7	0.7	3	0.8	0.8	70	10	200
40	0.2	11	0.9	0.8	0.9	4	0.8	0.8	80	10	200
40	0.2	13	1.1	1.0	1.0	4	0.9	0.9	100	10	250
40	0.3	15	1.2	1.1	1.2	5	1.0	1.0	110	10	250
40	0.4	17	1.3	1.3	1.4	5	1.2	1.2	125	10	300
45	0.4	18	1.4	1.4	1.6	5	1.4	1.4	135	18	350
55	0.4	20	1.5	1.5	1.8	5	1.4	1.4	150	18	400
60	0.4	18	1.6	1.4	2.0	5	0.8	0.8	140	10	400
60	0.4	18	1.7	1.4	2.0	5	0.8	0.8	140	10	350
60	0.4	17	1.7	1.3	2.0	5	0.8	0.8	125	10	350
60	0.4	14	1.7	1.2	2.0	6	0.8	0.8	110	10	350
40	0.4	15	1.3	1.1	1.4	5	1.2	1.2	110	18	300
45	0.4	15	1.4	1.2	1.6	5	1.3	1.3	115	18	350
50	0.4	16	1.4	1.2	1.8	5	1.3	1.3	120	18	350
50	0.4	15	1.5	1.2	2.0	5	1.3	1.3	115	18	350
55	0.4	13	1.5	1.0	2.0	5	0.8	0.8	100	18	350
55	0.4	13	1.5	1.0	2.0	5	0.8	0.8	100	18	300
55	0.4	13	1.5	1.0	2.0	5	0.8	0.8	90	18	300
55	0.4	13	1.5	1.0	2.0	6	0.8	0.8	80	10	300
60	0.8	15	1.8	+0.1	2.5	8	+0.4	+0.4	125	18	450
60	0.5	20	2.0	+0.5	2.5	6	+0.5	+0.5	150	18	450

CHART 2

NUTRITIONAL MENU-PLANNING GUIDE

(Values based on Average Servings)

	VEGETABLES AND FRUITS				PROTEIN FOODS			STARCHES	FATS
	Green and Yellow Vegetables	Citrus Fruits, Tomatoes, Raw Cabbage, Salad Greens	Potatoes	Other Vegetables and Fruits	Milk and Milk Products	Meat, Fish, Poultry, Eggs	Legumes (dried beans, peas, lentils, etc.)	Bread, Flour and Cereals	Butter and Oils
Calories (Energy)	x	x	xxx	x to xx	xx	xx	xxx	x to xx	xxx
Proteins	....	....	x	x	xx	xxx	xxx	x	....
Carbohydrates (Sugars and Starches)	x	x	xxx	x to xx	xx	....	xx to xxx	xx to xxx	....
Fats	....	....	....	....	x to xx	x to xx	x	....	xxx
Minerals Calcium	xxx	xxx[1]	x	x to xx	xxx	xx to xxx	xx	x	....

	1	2	3	4	5	6	7	8	9
Iron	xxx	xxx[1]	xx	x to xx	xxx	....	xx	x to xx	....
Phosphorus	x	....	xx	xx	x	xx	xxx	xx	....
Vitamins									
A	xxx	xxx	x	x to xx	x to xx	xx	x to xxx	x to xxx	xx
B-group	x	x to xx	x	....	x to xxx	x to xxx	....	x to xxx	....
C	xx to xxx	xxx	x	xx	....	xx to xxx	trace	....	trace
D[4]	....	....	....	....	irradiated xxx	xx[2] / xxx[3]	trace	....	trace
E[5]	x	x	x	....	x	x	....	x	xxx
Roughage	xx	xxx	xx	xx	....	xx	....	x	....
Water	xx	xxx	x	xx	xx to xxx	x	xx	....	....

Explanation: xxx excellent source
xx good source
x fair source
.... none or negligible quantity

[1]Salad greens only.
[2]Liver only.
[3]Red salmon only.
[4]Very few foods contain enough vitamin D to be of value unless they have been fortified with vitamin D concentrates. Direct sunshine is one of the main sources of this vitamin. Fish liver oils are satisfactory sources.
[5]Oils, whole grains, eggs, turnip greens.

CHART 3

FOOD ELEMENTS — WHAT THEY DO AND WHERE THEY ARE

PROTEINS: The chemical base of all living cells, and, therefore, essential in the growth and repair of bodily tissues; they also furnish some energy and heat.

Proteins are largely supplied by meat, fish, poultry, eggs and legumes (especially soybeans), by milk and milk products, and nuts.

CARBOHYDRATES (SUGARS AND STARCHES): The main source of fuel (calories), which the body converts into energy and heat.

Carbohydrates are largely supplied by sugar in all its forms (plain, honey, syrups, jams, fruits, etc.), by milk, and by all starchy foods, such as bread, cereals, potatoes, rice and starchy vegetables.

FATS: The source of fuel in highly concentrated form.

Most of the fats in our diet are supplied by butter, oils, cream and fat cheese, fat meat and fish, salad dressings and nuts.

MINERALS

CALCIUM: Essential in the formation of strong bones and teeth, and for normal lactation; aids blood clotting; an important factor in normal functioning of heart, nerves, and muscles, and in the regulation and co-ordination of other bodily functions.

Calcium is largely supplied by milk and milk products, eggs, shellfish, legumes, green leafy vegetables, molasses, bran, and whole-grain cereals.

PHOSPHORUS: An essential constituent of all living cells; indispensable in the work of making the energy of carbohydrates and fats available to the body; combined with calcium, in building bones and teeth; helps maintain the body's alkaline balance.

Phosphorus is largely supplied by milk and milk products, meat, fish, eggs, seafood, legumes, wheat germ and nuts.

IRON: Essential in forming hemoglobin (red blood cells) and in transporting oxygen.

Iron is largely supplied by lean meat, fish, poultry, eggs, liver, legumes, green leafy vegetables, bread, flour, and whole-grain cereals, potatoes and dried fruits.

Many other minerals are needed by the body to control the behavior of body fluids and tissues; they are widely distributed in foods containing calcium and iron. Among those minerals are copper, magnesium, manganese, potassium and sodium chloride (table salt).

VITAMINS

A: Essential for clear vision (especially in dim light) and for normal pregnancy and lactation; promotes normal growth and aids resistance to infection; a factor in normal functioning of glands.

Vitamin A is largely supplied by green and yellow vegetables, leafy green vegetables and tomatoes, liver, egg yolk and fish roe, butter and fortified margarine, milk and milk products, apricots and yellow fruits.

B-Group*

B_1:   Thiamin: Promotes normal growth and is a factor in the normal functioning of the nervous system; indispensable in the work of making the energy of carbohydrates available to the body; stimulates appetite.

B_1 is largely supplied by lean meat, especially pork, liver and other organ meats, milk and milk products, whole grains, legumes, green leafy vegetables, peas, beans and peanuts.

B_2:   Riboflavin: Promotes general health, vigor and growth; essential in maintaining the proper tone of the nervous and digestive systems.

B_2 is largely supplied by milk and milk products, the organ meats of beef, veal and pork, lean meat, eggs, and peanuts, green and yellow vegetables, and the germ portion of cereals.

Niacin: A factor in normal growth and health, digestion and skin function.

Niacin is largely supplied by liver and all meats, bread and whole grain cereals, legumes, yeast, milk and milk products, salmon, leafy green vegetables, mushrooms and peanuts.

C: Ascorbic Acid: Essential in strong tooth and bone formation and for healthy gums; a factor in normal growth, resistance to infection, and normal glandular function; helps to keep cell walls and blood vessels strong.

D: Essential in the body's utilization of calcium and phosphorus
      and their proper distribution in body fluids; indispensable
      for strong bone and tooth formation.
          Vitamin D is not largely distributed among foods. Milk that
      has been fortified with vitamin D, and red salmon are excellent
      sources.

E: Supplied by vegetable oils, whole grains, wheat germ, fish
      and liver, eggs, turnip greens.

   *To date, other members of the B-complex, i.e., B_6 and B_{12}, have
been identified. Good sources of B_6 are whole grains, wheat germ,
oils, legumes and muscle meat. Good sources of B_{12} are liver, also
brewer's yeast, kidneys, milk and wheat germ.

   Natural B-complex sources are brewer's yeast, liver, rice polish,
wheat germ and soybeans.

Vegetables From Store to Stove

FRESH VEGETABLE preparation does not start in the kitchen but in the store, for good quality is one of the essentials in getting full value. To buy wisely and economically, the homemaker will find the "Buying Guide" a help in proper selection. "Bargain" buying is often poor economy.

When the vegetables arrive in the kitchen, they must be handled with great care, for they are perishable. The food value of fresh vegetables decreases with the length and conditions of storage. Obviously, the ideal condition is one in which there is the least lag between the time the vegetable is picked and the time it appears on the table. As such an ideal condition is frequently impossible to attain, especially in larger communities, the homemaker has to avoid food losses by proper preparation and storage at home. Intelligent selection and wise buying otherwise fail in their purpose. Whatever vegetable is not used immediately must be properly stored. The "Storage Guide" gives practical suggestions for storing vegetables in the home.

Proper cleaning is essential, no matter what vegetable is being used. Do not be niggardly with either time, care or water in the cleaning of vegetables. Avoid tearing leafy vegetables; tears permit the water-soluble vitamins and minerals to escape into the water in the course of washing. If leaves are not torn, washing will not hurt them.

Since most vitamins and minerals lie directly beneath their skin, it is best to cook vegetables unpeeled. Turnips are the one exception to this rule, as their skin is bitter. Peel as thin as possible, if peel you must, and cook the peelings immediately to make

15

a vegetable stock. This stock can be used in a variety of ways, and thus losses of valuable food substances are avoided.

To be fresh, vegetables should never be prepared long in advance; while this is a primary rule for raw salads, it is almost as important for all cooked vegetables. Cooking develops the taste of vegetables, softens tough fibers, and makes starchy vegetables digestible—but only *if* vegetables are not overcooked. Cook just until tender. Avoid cooking more than is needed for one meal. Food losses occur when vegetables are cooked in too much water, or when too much cut surface is exposed to the water or the air. Therefore, cook vegetables whole rather than cut in pieces, and in their skins rather than peeled. As vitamins are destroyed by air, too frequent or too vigorous stirring should be avoided. High temperature is another enemy of vitamins, so that simmering is better than vigorous boiling, and a moderate oven is the best choice when vegetables are baked or broiled. Baking soda, too, destroys vitamins and should never be used in the cooking of vegetables.

Steaming, which is cooking in live steam or over boiling water—in a steamer or pressure cooker—is the best method because the least food losses occur. *Baking*, which is cooking in an oven by dry heat, and *broiling*, which is cooking over or under a flame at moderate temperatures, are excellent methods to develop flavor and preserve value; prolonged baking in a hot oven, however, should be avoided. *Panning*, which is cooking in a pan on top of the stove (usually in a heavy skillet), is a convenient way to prepare watery vegetables. *Boiling*, which is usually cooking in briskly boiling water, causes the greatest food losses, and should be avoided. However, *simmering*, which is cooking just below the boiling point of water, is kind to vegetables and therefore recommended. In the Cooking Guide for Fresh Vegetables, "boiling" means simmering. *Frying*, which is cooking in either shallow or deep fat, can attack vitamins if the fat's temperature is too high; however, frying adds calories to the dish and has a decided appetite appeal.

If properly prepared, vegetables retain their natural flavor and need only slight seasoning; *herbs and spices* always add zest and individuality. They should be used sparingly. An old herb rule says, "Be spendthrift in selecting herbs and miserly in using them."

For vegetables, the most commonly used herbs are basil, borage, celery, chives, chervil, fennel, marjoram, parsley, rosemary, sage, savory, thyme and water cress. Of spices: allspice, bay leaf, caraway seeds, cayenne pepper, celery seeds, chili powder, cumin, curry powder, ginger, mace, mustard (dry), nutmeg, paprika, red, white and black pepper and saffron. Capers, horseradish, juniper berries, olives, onions and green pepper may be used as condiments.

Dried or ground condiments should be purchased in small quantities and stored in tightly closed containers, as they lose their fragrance when exposed to the air. Fresh herbs can easily be grown in good earth in any garden; even the city homemaker can grow them in pots standing on the kitchen windowsill.

The recipes in this book suggest herbs and spices wherever it seems desirable. However, as seasoning is largely a matter of personal taste, the homemaker will frequently make up her own combinations. The "Seasoning Guide" tells which spices and herbs blend best with each vegetable.

The Salad Bowl

REFRESHING, crisp, and appetite-whetting salads know no season; the contents may vary with the time of the year, but a fresh salad should be served at least once and preferably twice every day. There is practically no vegetable which, in one form or another, cannot go into a salad. Moreover, fruits such as tart apples, grapefruit, or bananas, as well as cottage cheese balls, combine well with vegetables in a main-dish salad. Salads can easily be changed by varying dressings.

As most vegetables are low in calories, especially the green-leaved and watery types, salads are a boon for those with an eye to the scales. A low-calorie dressing will further restrict the calorie value of the salad. Salads are equally welcome to those endeavoring to put on weight rather than to lose it. For the latter, the salads should be made primarily of starchy vegetables, such as peas, beans, celery knobs and potatoes, and mixed with a rich dressing of mayonnaise or sour cream. This is an appetizing and easy way to sneak in extra calories.

Salads fill but do not stuff, which is one reason why they are hot weather favorites. Another reason to use raw salads liberally is that they provide a maximum of nutrition, for there is no such loss in food value as may occur in cooking. Still another important reason

18

is that leftover cooked vegetables are best used in a salad, thus avoiding reheating and additional loss in food values.

All varieties of lettuce, as well as cabbage, celery, chicory, escarole, fennel, green pepper, scallions, young spinach, tomatoes, water cress and avocados, are preferably served as raw salads. Very young beets, carrots, onions, kohlrabi and peas can also be served raw. All other vegetables can be used in salads only when cooked.

RAW VEGETABLE SALADS

There are a few rules to observe in successful preparation.

First and foremost is scrupulous, absolute cleanliness; a bit of grit can be as annoying in the mouth as in the eye, and a worm will ruin the best salad for any eater. Raw, crisp vegetables should be very crisp, not limp or wilted. If necessary, crisp vegetables in ice water for a few minutes before they are cut. After washing, drain all vegetables or shake almost dry.

Discard only such leaves of lettuce and other greens as are blemished; the dark outer leaves, which may be too tough to be eaten raw, make an excellent vegetable when cooked. Except when shredding the hard heads of lettuce, do not use a knife to cut green salads; rather tear with fingers into bite size. The soft varieties of lettuce must be handled lightly, for they wilt readily. Tomatoes slice easily if a sharp knife or a fine saw-toothed knife is used. Green peppers can be cut into thin strips or rings, or chopped fine. Cucumbers need not be peeled if sliced paper-thin and if the skin is not bitter. Also, they should never be salted and pressed out, as the loss of water makes them less digestible. Celery can be either cut into one-inch rings or

shredded coarsely. Onions can be cut into paper-thin
rings, chopped fine, or shredded. Other vegetables,
such as beets and carrots, are best shredded, either
long or short, on a fine shredder; carrots can also be
cut into thin strips.

Raw vegetables, with the exception of tomatoes and
cucumbers, should be mixed with the dressing
immediately before serving, and with the same exceptions, must not be kept from one meal to another.
Shredded vegetables are very delicate and quickly turn
pulpy; they lose in appearance, taste and food value
if handled with a heavy hand. Therefore, shred as near
as possible to eating time and sprinkle immediately
with a little oil and lemon juice.

COOKED VEGETABLE SALADS

Vegetables for use in a salad must not be cooked
so soft as to mash easily; either cube or slice to average
bite size. Unlike raw vegetables, cooked vegetables
gain by marinating, that is, being mixed with the dressing and allowed to stand at least one to two hours.
To save time, put dressing on a leftover vegetable while
it is still hot and put it, well-covered, in the refrigerator
to be used within twenty-four hours.

An attractive vegetable salad is the jellied mold or
the salad mousse, to be prepared ahead of serving time.

THE SALAD DRESSING

The dressing makes or ruins the salad. Oil, an acid
(either vinegar or lemon juice), salt and other seasonings (herbs, spices and condiments), and in some dressings, eggs or egg yolks, are the essential ingredients
of the salad dressing. The choice of salad oil is a matter
of individual taste; olive oil, corn, cottonseed, peanut,
sesame and soybean oil, or a mixture of them, are the

most commonly used. Of natural vinegars, wine or herb vinegars, especially tarragon, and also malt and cider vinegar are best, but they are not available everywhere; health-food stores carry a large variety of fine vinegars. A good vinegar can easily be prepared at home.

Dressings can be varied by different seasonings. If mayonnaise or sour cream is used as the dressing, it usually needs a little lemon juice or vinegar to make it thinner.

A jar of French dressing and one of mayonnaise in the refrigerator will save time and work. Some French or similar dressings separate on standing and must be well shaken before use. Dressings containing sour cream do not keep well and should never be stored long.

The low-calorie dressing with mineral oil as an ingredient should be avoided, as mineral oil is an enemy to some vitamins. Buttermilk, which is low in calories and tasty, makes a very adequate substitute for the usual salad oil.

The seasoning of a salad dressing depends in part on personal taste and in part on the vegetables used. Bland vegetables need slightly higher seasoning than strong-flavored ones. The "Seasoning Guide" tells what condiments, herbs and spices may be used with what vegetables.

Add the thoroughly mixed dressing to raw vegetables just before serving; mix well, but lightly, so as not to crush the vegetable, especially when leaves are very tender or vegetable is shredded.

To serve: arrange the salad with an eye to color, but avoid an artificial appearance. Radishes cut into roses, curled celery and carrots, shoestring carrots, or stuffed olives and pickles lend a festive touch. Finely cut chives, parsley, dill or mint, most easily done with a scissors, can be added either before or after the dressing is applied. Sliced eggs or egg wedges, too, make an attractive garnishing.

Salad can be served in individual portions, especially if it is to replace a soup or juice, but the most convenient way to serve it is in a shallow wooden bowl with a wooden fork and spoon. Some like the taste of garlic or special herbs. If so, rub the wooden bowl with a cut clove of garlic or special herbs before mixing the salad in it. This imparts the taste to the salad without being too obvious. If other than wooden bowls are used, they should be chilled before use.

Kitchen Shortcuts, Pots And Pans

These are all designed to save you time and steps in tasteful vegetable preparation.

Asparagus and Broccoli: Don't be reckless and throw away your old percolator; it's just the thing for steaming asparagus and broccoli.

Cabbage: Two or three slices of stale bread act like a magic wand in removing cabbage odor, both from the cabbage and from the kitchen. Place bread—wrapped in cheesecloth—over cabbage, cover, and cook.

Cauliflower: Double the yield of a head of cauliflower by cooking the stalks. Trim off leafy part and ends and cook along with the cauliflower. Serve cut or chopped, creamed, scalloped, or au gratin.

If you intend to cream, cook in half milk, half water, and use liquid for the white sauce.

Celery: Some markets sell, in bunches or by the pound, the stalks which they trim off celery, a very much cheaper way to buy celery for cooking.

Corn: A dry, small and stiff brush will readily remove the silk from corn.

A sharp knife and a skewer help when cutting corn off a hot cob. Hold upright, enter skewer, slice downward.

Throw away the husks of corn only after they have served as a cover when roasting. This holds good for both indoor and outdoor roasting.

Eggs: When beating egg whites, make a little into more by adding—before beating—¼ teaspoonful of cold water and a pinch of salt for each egg white.

A bit of yolk, if it drops into the white, can be popped out again with the edge of the eggshell or the corner of a damp cloth.

Kitchen Bouquets: They do not stand in flower pots, but swim in soups, tied in little bags. One or two sprigs of parsley, one sprig each of thyme and marjoram, and ½ bay leaf—all except bay leaf fresh and fragrant—and be sure to remove before you serve.

Lemons: More juice can be squeezed out of a lemon if it is first heated in a moderate oven for five minutes.

When storing part of a lemon, cover exposed surface, and store in refrigerator.

Save lemon rinds; they are useful in removing kitchen odors and stains from your hands.

Onions: Peel under water if you dislike tears. For onion juice minus grief, sprinkle surface with salt and scrape with a knife.

Store part of an onion, if you must, only in a small jar with tight screw top in the refrigerator.

Onion Rings and Other Things: Peel the onion; hold tight at stem end of a wooden board and chop downward with a sharp knife; always start at blossom end.

Take the bite out of onions: heat fat, add sliced or chopped onions and cook gently until soft but pale, not brown. This is known as panning.

Out of the sewing box and into the kitchen! Use scissors not only on cloth, but also on chives, parsley and dill. It's quick and easy.

Potatoes: For fluffy mashed potatoes, add a stiffly beaten egg white; if you like them creamy, add hot milk. In any case, beat hard.

A little flour sprinkled on raw slices of potato before frying helps to keep them crisp.

Rice: Do not wash rice; pick over and rub between two clean towels or shake well in the flour sifter.

One teaspoon of lemon juice to each quart of cooking water makes rice fluffier and whiter.

If you don't have a special method of your own to cook your rice: boil in four times more water than rice; drain and "wash" in running hot water after cooking. Steam for a minute or two afterwards.

Seasonings: You'll be surprised what a bit of caraway seed, bay leaf and marjoram will do to a steamed vegetable. Keep a little bag filled with them handy, use as needed, dry and use again.

This is not the only role of caraway seeds; moisten and chop and add to a dish.

Chopped chives, if allowed to cook, will bite; add at the last moment.

Green peppers are filled to bursting with vitamins, and a little chopped pepper adds a lot to a dish. Since it is a pity to kill the vitamins by long cooking, a few minutes are enough.

Spaghetti, Macaroni and Noodles: Don't be disheartened if your pot boils over when you put the cover on boiling spaghetti. Next time, add one tablespoonful of oil to the cooking water, cover, and see what happens.

Sour Cream: If sour cream is still a stranger, cultivate its acquaintance. It does wonders for a creamed dish when used instead of white sauce.

Tomatoes: Ripe tomatoes peel easily if dropped into boiling water for a minute. Or rub all over with dull edge of knife. Slit skin at blossom end and peel toward stem.

Turnips: Turnips must be peeled, as their skin is bitter. Slice and peel the slices. Saves time and your temper.

To Blanch: Strong flavored vegetables become genteel when plunged into slightly salted boiling water for two or three minutes. If it's too hot to do this, let them stand in cold salted water for thirty minutes.

To Chop–A Trick: A medium-sized sharp knife and a wooden board are all you need to chop parsley, onions or mushrooms. Hold point of knife firmly on the board with your left hand, grasp handle on the right and swing horizontally in half circle, chopping as you go.

To Dice Vegetables: This sounds more difficult than it is, but when done right, it looks very professional. Take a sharp knife in the right hand, vegetable in the left, place on wooden board and slice lengthwise, both horizontally and vertically, in half-inch slices; hold on for dear life. And slice again crosswise. Keep your slices even.

To Fry in Deep Fat: Don't try any marriages in the frying kettle! Each time it's used, the fat should be pure as the driven snow. It's not hard to do, either. Cook a few slices of raw potatoes or stale bread in the fat for 10 minutes, after you have used it. Strain through a thick cloth, and there you are!

And if you don't like to be spattered with fat, fill the kettle only two-thirds full. A frying basket and a long-handled skimmer help, too.

A thermometer is your best friend when it comes to deep-fat frying. And don't forget: food must be at room temperature, never ice cold.

To "Butter" Bread Crumbs: Buttered bread crumbs add oomph to a lot of dishes. Heat the butter in a heavy skillet, add crumbs and stir briskly until the butter is absorbed. As for bread cubes, crisp and buttery is the word.

To Grease a Baking Dish: Use your fingers to grease a baking dish. Just make sure that there are no neglected spots. A bit of paper serves the same purpose: no brush to wash, no greasy pot to clean.

To Fill a Baking Dish: Allow for expansion—fill only two-thirds full—especially if milk or eggs are used in the recipes. This will prevent a mess in the oven.

Baking Dish from Cold to Hot: Unless it's freezer-to-oven ware, ice-cold baking dishes don't take kindly to a hot oven, so don't pop them straight from the refrigerator into the oven. Let stand in the kitchen a while, or if you are in a hurry, set the dish over steaming water for a few minutes.

To Keep Vegetables in Color: White and red vegetables will retain their color if a few drops of lemon juice or vinegar are added to the cooking water; green vegetables stay green if cooking water is salted, or one or two lettuce leaves are cooked with the vegetable. Yellow vegetables are stubborn—need no crutch.

To Keep Vegetables Hot: An old trick but good. Don't get cross if you have to keep vegetables hot beyond their appointed time just because Jim is late. Wrap the pot in several thicknesses of paper towels. This keeps heat in with a minimum of effort. Potatoes in their skins, of course, should be drained dry before being wrapped.

To Modify Strong Flavor of Vegetables: If you dislike remarks about kitchen odors, blanch strong vegetables (Brussels sprouts, cabbage, cauliflower and kale) or remove the condensation which accumulates on the cover by wiping it off several times during the cooking.

To Stretch Vegetables in an Emergency: The unexpected guest need cause no terror. A large potato, raw and peeled, is quickly grated into a vegetable. Use glass or plastic grater. Bring to a quick boil and serve. See how the quantity increases magically.

The Kitchen Bowl: Stays put, if placed on a damp cloth.

The Salad Bowl: Treat your wooden salad bowl with kid gloves; do not soak. A clean cloth, wrung out in hot soapy water, is all the water that the bowl will stand. Dry with paper towel, polish with oiled cloth—till tomorrow.

The Salad Dressing Jar: Don't be stingy when mixing salad dressing. Use a large enough jar so it won't spill over when you stir vigorously.

Pots and Pans: Like the well-dressed woman, the well-equipped kitchen is a question of personal choice and experience, rather than money. Don't let other workers have a monopoly on efficient tools. A sensibly equipped kitchen does much to cut down work.

An asbestos mat avoids scorched pots and scorched vegetables, saving your temper and your pennies, while a larger-sized asbestos mat is fine to save working surfaces from burns caused by hot pots. It's amazing in how many ways baking dishes and casseroles, especially those with covers, can be used if you put your mind to it: not only for baking, but for keeping vegetables hot while serving, or for reheating. Not number but size and quality are the important thing when it comes to pots and pans. Use tight-fitting covers by all means, and don't forget the heavy skillets, or the round-bottomed double boiler. But do forget chipped enamelware. A few knives—small, medium and large—are essential, and all must be sharp. Also a spatula or two; a wooden bowl and chopping knife; a rotary egg beater and a funnel; a soup ladle, strainers, some wooden spoons with nice long handles; and a shredder or shredders, best of glass or plastic—all belong in the well-run kitchen. And a shiny clean sink with a rubber stopper, to wash your vegetables!

The economical housewife may also include a frying basket and a skimmer, a food mill, a pressure cooker and an electric blender; she will find plenty of use for these practical tools.

Don't measure quantities with your eyes: use standard measuring cups and spoons. They are the little things that make for cooking success.

PART TWO

What And How—
In A Nutshell

Here—in a nutshell—is practical information the homemaker needs, from the moment she sits down to plan meals to the moment the family sits down to eat.

THE DAILY MENU PLANNER
Kinds and quantities of foods which must be eaten each day.

VEGETABLE GROUPS IN THE DAILY MENU PLANNER
A complete list of vegetables in each group.

THE BUYING GUIDE
How much to buy and what to look for when buying vegetables.

THE CLEANING GUIDE
How to wash vegetables.

THE STORAGE GUIDE
How to care for vegetables.

THE COOKING GUIDE
A step-by-step description of how to cook vegetables.

THE SEASONING GUIDE
What herbs and spices can be used with each vegetable.

The Daily Menu Planner

THE DAILY MENU PLANNER
(U.S. Government Nutrition Guide)

Food Groups	Minimum Average Servings	Your Choice
Green and Yellow Vegetables	one or more of each	raw or cooked
Citrus Fruit; *Tomato, Raw Greens or Cabbage*	one or more of each	preferably raw or as juice
Potatoes and Other Vegetables; Fruit (including Berries)	one potato; one each of vegetable and fruit	cooked; fruit also as juice; rice as alternate
Milk and Milk Products	Teenagers: 4 cups+ Adults: 2 cups + Pregnancy: 3 cups+	fluid or cultured; part as cheese or ice cream
Meat, Poultry, Fish, and Eggs; *Legumes (Soybeans, Dried Beans and Peas, Lentils)* Nuts; Peanut Butter	one of meat or meat alternate; 3 to 4 eggs per week	include eggs used in cooking as part of average weekly servings
Bread and Cereals	three of bread; one of cereal	best natural wholegrain; or enriched
Fats	as needed	butter, oils
Water	6 or more glasses	
Coffee or Tea	as and if desired	herbal teas as alternate
Sugars	as and if desired	brown sugar and honey as alternates
Any Other Foods? (optional)	according to personal preference	desserts and soft drinks

Vegetable Groups

in the Daily Menu Planner

GREEN AND YELLOW VEGETABLES: raw, cooked, quick-frozen or canned

Green Vegetables
- Artichokes, French or globe
- Asparagus
- Beans, snap
- Beet greens or tops
- Broccoli
- Brussels sprouts
- Cabbage, green varieties
- Celery
- Collards
- Fennel
- Kale
- Lettuce
- Okra
- Onions, green (scallions)
- Peas
- Peppers, green
- Soybeans, fresh green
- Spinach
- Swiss Chard
- Turnip greens

Yellow Vegetables
- Beans, wax
- Carrots
- Corn, yellow
- Pumpkins
- Rutabagas
- Squash, yellow varieties
- Sweet potatoes
- Yams

"Wild" Greens
- Chicory
- Curly dock
- Dandelion
- Lamb's Quarters
- Mustard
- Sorrel

SALAD GREENS or TOMATOES (raw, cooked or as juice); *GREENS* as salad

Salad Greens

Celery		
Chicory	or	*Raw Cabbage*, all green varieties
Endive		
Escarole	or	*Tomatoes*
Lettuce, all varieties		
Parsley	or	*Soybean Sprouts*
Peppers, green		
Scallions		

POTATOES, AND OTHER VEGETABLES; fresh, quick-frozen or canned

Potatoes
  White (Irish)

Other Vegetables

Artichokes, Jerusalem	Lima Beans
Beets	Mushrooms
Cabbage, red	Onion, dry varieties
Cauliflower	Parsnips
Celeriac (Knob Celery)	Radishes
Chayotes	Salsify (Oysterplant)
Corn, white	Sauerkraut
Cucumbers	Squash, summer
Dasheens	Turnips, white
Eggplant	Vegetable Marrow
Kohlrabi	Zucchini
Leeks	

LEGUMES or NUTS:

Legumes or *Nuts*

DRIED BEANS
  Kidney Beans
  Lima Beans
  Navy Beans
  Pinto Beans
  Soybeans

      Almonds
      Beechnuts
      Brazilnuts
      Chestnuts
      Cocoanuts
      Filberts (Hazelnuts)
      Pecans
      Walnuts

DRIED PEAS
  Black-eye Peas
  Cowpeas
  Field Peas
  Split Peas

LENTILS

PEANUTS
  and Peanut Butter

CASHEW NUTS

Buying Guide For Fresh Vegetables

(All quantities are for *four average servings;*
cup measurements are approximate)

ALWAYS BUY vegetables as fresh as possible. Obviously, when in season they are both cheaper and fresher. As you select them, avoid unnecessary handling.

Because all leafy and watery vegetables are highly perishable, it is inadvisable to buy ahead in large quantities. Also, it is poor economy to buy wilted, limp, bruised, underripe or overripe vegetables, for their food value decreases in proportion to loss of freshness. Storage space permitting, winter vegetables may be bought in larger quantities.

The following are the things to look for and the things to avoid in buying vegetables:

ARTICHOKES, FRENCH OR GLOBE: Compact, heavy, plump globes with green, fleshy leaves; the medium- and large-sized artichokes have the fleshiest leaves.

Avoid: Globes that look withered, have outward spreading leaves with hard or curly tips, or brownish, brown, or badly spotted leaves.

Quantity: 1 artichoke per serving.

—JERUSALEM: Sound, smooth and reasonably clean.
Avoid: Blemished, bruised or injured tubers, or with dark, discolored spots.
Quantity: 1 to 1½ pounds.

ASPARAGUS: Firm and tender, compact tips, brittle stalks; all the stalks in the bunch should be fairly uniform in thickness, straight, and almost entirely green.
Avoid: Wilted appearance, spreading tips, tough or spongy stalks of brownish or yellowish color.
Quantity: 1 large bunch (about 2 pounds).

AVOCADOS OR ALLIGATOR PEARS: Heavy, fairly firm, medium-sized, bright fresh green in color.
Avoid: Bruised or injured fruit, with dark, sunken spots, or broken skins.
Quantity: Depends on use, usually ½ pear per serving.

BEANS, LIMA (FRESH): Pods clean, dark green in color, firm, and well filled. Shelled beans should be tender, with green or greenish-white skin.
Avoid: Dirty, shriveled, spotted, or flabby pods, and beans with hard and white skins.
Quantity: About 3 pounds in pods—2½ to 3 cups, cooked.

—FAVA OR FABA: Similar to lima beans, only rounder and with somewhat larger and thicker pods. Shelled beans thicker and more globular in shape and with a thick, tough skin.
Quantity: About 3 pounds in pods—2½ to 3 cups, cooked.

—SNAP (STRING): Baby beans—clean, firm but tender. Mature beans—clean and crisp, snapping readily when broken; soft green in color, and without blemishes or insect injury.

Avoid: Discolored, wilted, shriveled, tough, woody, stringy, or blemished beans.

Quantity: About 1½ pounds—3½ to 4 cups, cut and cooked.

—SOY, FRESH GREEN: See Soybeans, Fresh Green.

—WAX (YELLOW): Clean, firm but tender, snapping readily when broken; pale yellow in color and without blemishes.

Avoid: Discolored, wilted, shriveled, stringy, blemished, or watery beans.

Quantity: About 1 ½ pounds — 3 ½ to 4 cups, cut and cooked.

BEETS: Smooth, undamaged, preferably with fresh tops (which can be used as greens), and of medium size. Wilted or damaged tops do not necessarily imply poor quality of beets.

Avoid: Rough, ridged, deeply cracked, flabby, or shriveled beets.

Quantity: If mature and without tops—about 1 ½ pounds; if young—about 8 medium beets (usually 4 beets to 1 bunch) — about 3 cups, cut and cooked.

BROCCOLI: Compact bud clusters, darkish or purplish green in color; tender, firm stalks, and a minimum of large leaves. An occasional open blossom does not indicate overmaturity.

Avoid: Loose, yellowish flowerets, woody or flabby stalks, and wilted leaves.

Quantity: 1 bunch (about 2 ½ pounds) — 4 to 4 ½ cups, broken into flowerets and cooked.

BRUSSELS SPROUTS: Firm, crisp, light green in color and uniform in size.

Avoid: Smudged, dirty or puffy sprouts, with yellowed or riddled leaves.

Quantity: 1 quart basket (about 1 ½ pounds) — 3 ½ to 4 cups, cooked.

CABBAGE: All varieties of cabbage should be firm and heavy for their size. Color and solidity vary with variety.

Avoid: Cabbage with yellowed leaves, injured, soft or puffy heads; in compact varieties, those heads whose leaves do not cling to head of cabbage.

Quantity: 1 medium head (1 ½ to 2 pounds) — about 4 cups, cut and cooked — 10 servings, if served raw.

CARROTS: Clean, firm, smooth, regular-shaped, and of bright color; if bought with tops, bright green and unwilted leaves.

Avoid: Blemished, shriveled, or soft carrots, or those that are too large or of poor color.

Quantity: 1 or 2 bunches (about 1 ½ pounds) depending on size and age of carrot — 3 to 3 ½ cups, cut and cooked.

CAULIFLOWER: Compact, firm, creamy-white in color and of a velvety appearance, in a heavy cluster of unwilted dark green leaves.

Avoid: Blemished or bruised, loose heads, with dark spots, and wilted or yellowed leaves.

Quantity: 1 medium head (about 2 ½ pounds) — 3 ½ to 4 cups, broken into flowerets and cooked.

CELERIAC: See Celery Knob.

CELERY, GREEN OR WHITE: Crisp, unblemished, compact, brittle stalks that snap easily leaves of good fresh color; firm hearts, if sold by bunch.

Avoid: Bruised or blemished stalks with wilted, discolored leaves, or seed stems.

Quantity: 1 large or 2 small bunches (about 2 pounds) depending on kind of celery and number of stalks or hearts to a bunch — about 3 ½ cups, cut and cooked.

—KNOB: Solid knobs, heavy for their size, and with a minimum or blemishes.

Avoid: Knobs with badly discolored or soft spots.

Quantity: 2 medium heads (1 ½ to 2 pounds) — about 4 cups, cut and cooked.

CHARD, SWISS: Tender, unwilted leaves and stalks, dark green leaves, pale green stalks.

Avoid: Wilted, yellowish leaves and rubbery stalks.

Quantity: 1 large or 2 small bunches (about 2 pounds) — 3 to 3 ½ cups, cooked.

CHAYOTES: A pear-shaped vegetable of the cucumber family with a single large edible seed, resembling both squash and cucumber; flesh tender and of delicate flavor.

Quantity: 2 to 3 medium (1 to 1 ½ pounds).

CHESTNUTS: Firm, dry, dark brown in color, and shiny.

Avoid: Moist chestnuts with soft spots.

Quantity: 1 ½ pounds, or depending on use.

CHICORY: See Endive, French.

COLLARDS: Clean, crisp, dark green in color.

Avoid: Wilted, yellowish, or worm-eaten leaves.

Quantity: About 2 pounds.

CORN, SWEET—WHITE OR YELLOW: Fresh, green husks, full ears and milky kernels.

Avoid: Dry, yellowed husks, signs of worm damage, or ears only partially grown.

Quantity: 1 ear per serving, or depending on use. 1 ear — ¼ to ½ cup kernel corn, cooked, depending on size of cob and age of corn.

CUCUMBERS: Firm, straight, of regular shape, and deep green in color; if very young, somewhat rough-textured.

Avoid: Shriveled, badly misshapen cucumbers that are soft in spots, and of a dull, yellowish color.

Quantity: For cooking, 2 to 3 medium (1 to 1 ½ pounds) — about 3 ½ cups, cut and cooked; for salad, 1 to 2 medium.

DANDELION GREENS: Both the wild and cultivated varieties are on the market in early spring. Tender leaves of fresh, green color.

Avoid: Wilted, flabby, tough leaves, or leaves with seed stems or blossoms.

Quantity: 1 ½ to 2 pounds — about 2 cups, cooked.

DASHEENS: A tuber similar in composition to the potato, with a chestnutlike taste. The young leaves can be used like other greens.

Quantity: About 1 pound.

EGGPLANT: Firm, unbruised, heavy for size, and of an even, glossy, dark purple color.

Avoid: Shriveled, bruised eggplant, with dark brown spots or large blemishes.

Quantity: 1 large or 2 small (about 2 pounds) — 4 to 4 ½ cups, cut and cooked.

ENDIVE, CURLY: Crisp, tender, feathery loose head of narrow, finely divided green leaves shading to a creamy heart.

Avoid: Coarse, browning leaves and wilted appearance.

Quantity: 2 medium heads, or depending on use.

—FRENCH (BLANCHED OR WITLOOF CHICORY): Compact bud of folded, almost white leaves forming a small, solid elongated head.

Avoid: Wilted, discolored and bruised endive.

Quantity: 1 to 1½ pounds if cooked, or depending on use in salads.

ESCAROLE: Tender, broad and twisted leaves shading from dark green to creamy-white midribs.

Avoid: Wilted heads, damaged leaves, and signs of rot.

Quantity: 1 medium head, or depending on use.

FENNEL (FINOCHIO) Tastes strongly of anise; can be found in most Italian vegetable markets.

Avoid: Bruised and blemished fennel with dark spots, which are an indication of rot.

Quantity: 1 ½ pounds.

GARLIC: Sound, plump, unbroken, and with dry skin.

Avoid: Soft, spongy, dirty, or sprouting garlic.

Quantity: Depends on use.

"GREENS" (WILD) Chicory, curly dock, lamb's quarters, mustard, sorrel, etc., can be found in some vegetable markets in early spring. Beet and turnip tops are also sometimes sold separately as greens.

Fresh, young, tender or crisp leaves of good bright color.

Avoid: Dirty, wilted, very large leaves with coarse stems or insect injuries, or with seed stems or blossoms.

Quantity: 1 ½ to 2 pounds — about 2 cups, cooked.

KALE: Clean, crisp, and dark to bluish-green in color; in winter, sometimes brownish.

Avoid: Wilted, yellowish leaves; examine carefully for plant lice.

Quantity: 1 ½ to 2 pounds — about 2 cups, cooked.

KNOB CELERY: See Celery Knob.

KOHLRABI:Firm heads, small or medium in size, with fresh, pale green leaves.

Avoid: Cut or bruised knobs and wilted leaves.

Quantity: 1 ½ pounds, 4 to 8 knobs (1 large or 2 small bunches) — 3 to 3 ½ cups, cut and cooked.

LEEKS: Unblemished, dark green tops with white bulb and neck.

Avoid: Bruised, yellowed or wilted tops, and damaged necks.

*Quantity:*1 large bunch (4 to 6 large, or 8 to 10 small leeks).

LETTUCE: Compactness, color, and solidity depend on the variety. All varieties, however, should have crisp and tender leaves.

Avoid: Lettuce with discolored, broken or wilted leaves, and signs of rot, or seed stems.

Quantity: Depends on variety and use.

MUSHROOMS: White, unbroken, unblemished, firm-fleshed heads, and firm stems.

Avoid: Shriveled, discolored, broken mushrooms and flabby stems.

Quantity: 1 to 1 ½ pounds, depending on use.

OKRA (GUMBO): Clean, long or short pods, firm to the touch, and fresh white or green in color; tender, snapping easily when broken.
Avoid: Shriveled, discolored, or dried-out pods.
Quantity: 1 to 1 ½ pounds.

ONIONS, DRY: Size, color and shape depend on variety. All varieties should be well shaped, with dry outer skins and thin necks, if any at all.
Avoid: Bruised, blemished, or sprouting onions, or those that are moist around the neck.
Quantity: 1 to 1 ½ pounds, depending on use — 3 to 3 ½ cups, cut and cooked.

—SCALLIONS: Immature, green onions, pulled while tops are green and onion part still undeveloped.
Unblemished, fresh green tops, medium-sized necks, and slightly bulbous at the base.
Avoid: Bruised, wilted or yellowed scallions, or with damaged necks.
Quantity: 2 bunches, or depending on use.

OYSTERPLANT: See Salsify.

PARSLEY: Crisp, unwilted, deep green in color, and free from dirt.
Avoid: Badly wilted and yellowish leaves.
Quantity: Depends on variety and use.

PARSNIPS: Clean, firm, smooth-skinned, regular in shape, and not too large.
Avoid: Shriveled, flabby parsnips, and those that are too large or misshapen.
Quantity: 4 medium (1 to 1 ½ pounds) — about 3 ½ cups, cut and cooked.

PEAS: Smooth, firm, full pods; peas tender and sweet in taste.

Avoid: Pods that are dull in color, wilted, blemished, or damp.

Quantity: 2 ½ to 3 pounds, in pods — 2 ½ to 3 cups, cooked.

PEPPERS, GREEN: Firm, well-shaped, thick-fleshed, and shiny deep green in color.

Avoid: Flabby or misshapen peppers, with blemishes or soft spots.

Quantity: Depends on use (4 large for stuffing).

POTATOES, SWEET: See Sweet Potatoes.

—WHITE (IRISH): Sound, smooth-skinned, shallow-eyed, and reasonably clean. When sold in bulk, they are usually graded. New potatoes are frequently sold unwashed.

Avoid: Bruised, wilted, leathery, cut, or otherwise injured potatoes.

Quantity: 4 to 6 medium, or 1 ½ pounds new potatoes.

RADISHES, RED OR WHITE: Hard, clean, well-formed, bright red or white in color; red radishes preferably small, white radishes preferably medium-sized; unwilted leaves with small, crisp center leaves.

Avoid: Discolored, blemished radishes, or those that are spongy to the touch.

Quantity: Depends on use.

ROMAINE: A type of lettuce with coarser, elongated leaves.

Crisp and fairly firm, compact heads; leaves of fresh green color.

Avoid: Romaine with purplish tinge on outer edges of leaves, and signs of rot.

Quantity: 2 medium heads.

RUTABAGAS: See Turnips, Yellow.

SALSIFY (OYSTERPLANT) Smooth, evenly tapering, firm, and small or medium-sized.

Avoid: Flabby, shriveled, or misshapen salsify.

Quantity: 1 large bunch, or 1 to 1 ½ pounds (6 to 8 roots) — about 2 ½ cups, cut and cooked.

SCALLIONS: See Onions

SOYBEANS, FRESH GREEN: Clean, yellowish-green to green pods, firm, and well-filled.

Avoid: Dirty, shriveled, flabby, yellow pods.

Quantity: 1 ½ to 2 pounds, in pods — about 2 cups, cooked.

—SPROUTS: A year-round vegetable that may be used raw or cooked. On sale in stores catering to the Chinese; also in quick-frozen form and cans.

Tender, crisp, of light color, sprouts 2 to 3 inches long.

Avoid: Darkened, bluish sprouts that have lost their crispness.

Quantity: About 2 cups, or depending on use.

SPINACH: See "Greens."

SQUASH, ACORN (DES MOINES): Hard, regular in shape, and unblemished.

Avoid: Blemished or bruised squash, or with spots soft to the touch.

Quantity: ½ medium or 1 small per serving, depending on size.

—HUBBARD (WINTER): Hard, free from blemishes, and heavy for size.

Avoid: Squash which is bruised or has spots soft to the touch.

Quantity: 2 to 2 ½ pounds.

—VEGETABLE MARROW: Firm, unbruised, slightly glossy, dark green in color.

Avoid: Shriveled, flabby or blemished marrow.

Quantity: 2 to 3 medium (1 ½ to 2 pounds) — about 2 cups, cut and cooked.

—YELLOW (SUMMER): Firm but not hard, preferably with rind tender enough to puncture easily; fairly heavy for size.

Avoid: Squash that is flabby, bruised, or blemished. Squash with hard rind is usually stringy.

Quantity: About 2 pounds, 6 to 10 small, or 3 to 4 medium — 3 to 4 cups, cut and cooked.

—ZUCCHINI (ITALIAN SQUASH): Similar to vegetable marrow but smaller in size. Smaller and medium-sized zucchini are better than the large.

Avoid: Shriveled, blemished zucchini with spots that are soft to the touch.

Quantity: 2 to 3 medium (1 ½ to 2 pounds).

SWEET POTATOES: Firm, plump, tapering at the ends, and smooth-skinned.

Avoid: Sweet potatoes that are damp, have soft spots, other blemishes, attached rootlets, or are too irregular in shape.

Quantity: 4 medium (about 1 pound), or depending on use.

—YAMS: Somewhat darker in color than sweet potatoes, and of different shape. Dark blotches do not indicate poor quality.

Avoid: Very large yams and defects similar to sweet potatoes.

Quantity: 4 medium (about 1 pound), or depending on use.

SWISS CHARD: See Chard, Swiss.

TOMATOES, RED and YELLOW: Ripe, well-formed, plump, smooth-skinned and of even color. Depth of color varies with variety. Those showing growth-cracks should be bought only for immediate use.

Avoid: Misshapen tomatoes, or those that are bruised or otherwise blemished.

Quantity: 1 or 2 per serving (1 to 1 ½ pounds), or depending on use —2 to 3 cups, cooked.

TURNIPS, WHITE: Firm, smooth-skinned, with a minimum of leaf scars around the crown and few roots. When sold with tops, leaves should be crisp, tender, and fresh in color.

Avoid: Shriveled turnips with soft spots, or those that are overgrown (light in weight for size), or with wilted or yellowed leaves.

To make sure that turnip is not stringy, puncture with a finger nail; if incision remains dry, the turnip is stringy.

Quantity: 2 bunches (1 ½ to 2 pounds) — 4 cups, cut and cooked.

—YELLOW (RUTABAGAS): Larger in size than white turnips and never sold with tops, but otherwise the same as white turnips.

Quantity: 2 small (1 ½ to 2 pounds) — about 4 cups, cut and cooked.

VEGETABLE MARROW: See Squash.

WATER CRESS: Tender, crisp, glossy, deep green in color.

Avoid: Wilted water cress with shriveled, or yellowish leaves.

Quantity: 1 bunch, or depending on use.

YAMS: See Sweet Potatoes.

ZUCCHINI: See Squash.

Cleaning Guide

LEAFY VEGETABLES AND "GREENS": These must be thoroughly clean, whether stored or used immediately.

Pick over and discard all wilted and decayed leaves. Avoid tearing leaves, as tears allow water-soluble food substances to escape.

Wash in several cold waters without soaking. Adding 1 or 2 tablespoons of salt to the first water helps to remove dirt more quickly. Wash "greens" by dipping up and down in several waters; or cleanse leaf by leaf in running water.

Drain in colander after washing; if to be stored, drain and shake almost dry.

ROOT AND OTHER VEGETABLES: Wash and scrub with a small, firm brush, preferably under running water. Remove all eyes, rootlet and blemishes.

THOSE VEGETABLES that need not be washed before storing should merely have surface dirt removed. Then thorough cleaning is in order before use.

Storage Guide

Fresh vegetables deteriorate rapidly, and much of their food value is lost if they are stored too long or improperly. Some vegetables must be washed before refrigerator storage; others may be stored in the refrigerator without washing, while still others need only be stored in a cool, dark and dry place. All vegetables kept in the refrigerator must be placed in the lower part, in storage drawer, crisper, hydrator, well-covered bowl, food bag, or glass jar, or wrapped in plastic bag or slightly damp cloth. Avoid packing too tightly, as this causes bruising and early decay. Vegetables should never come in contact with freezing unit or ice.

FRESH VEGETABLES TO BE WASHED AND STORED IN THE REFRIGERATOR: Leafy vegetables should be shaken as dry as possible before storing. Root and other vegetables are best washed with a firm, not too stiff brush. The leaves of root vegetables, such as beets, carrots, kohlrabi, radishes and turnips, must be cut off the roots, leaving two to three inches of stem. Do not discard the tops that have been cut off; wash carefully and cook immediately. All "tops" are good as a soup stock; some even make a delicious vegetable. In winter, all root vegetables in the following list do not necessarily have to be stored refrigerated; they can be stored in any cool place:

Beets
Carrots
Collards
Lettuce and all Salad and "Wild" Greens

Parsley
Radishes
Spinach
Swiss Chard

FRESH VEGETABLES TO BE STORED IN THE REFRIGERATOR WITHOUT PRELIMINARY WASHING:

Artichokes (French or globe)
Avocados
Beans (Snap, Wax and Soy- beans)
Broccoli
Brussels Sprouts
Cauliflower
Celery (Green and White)
Cucumbers
Eggplant
Fennel
Kale

Leeks
Mushrooms
Okra
Peppers (Green)
Scallions
Squash (Summer, Vegetable Marrow, Zucchini)
Soybean sprouts will keep refrigerated for two to three days, depending on freshness when stored

FRESH VEGETABLES TO BE STORED IN A DRY, COOL AND DARK PLACE (not in the refrigerator and without preliminary washing):

Artichokes (Jerusalem)
Cabbage (all varieties)
Celery (Knob)
Chayotes
Dasheens
Kohlrabi

Onions (all dry varieties)
Parsnips
Potatoes (Irish, Sweet Pota- toes and Yams)
Pumpkin
Salsify (Oysterplant)
Turnips (White)

CORN, LIMA BEANS AND PEAS: Very easily lose their flavor and texture when stored too cold and too long.

TOMATOES: Rather sensitive to cold; unless very ripe, it is best to keep them in a dark, cool place and to chill them just before serving.

WINTER VEGETABLES: For storing, select fully grown vegetables, dry and sound, in good condition, and free from cuts, bruises and blemishes. The storage place should be cool but not so cold as to cause freezing and not too dry. If winter vegetables are to be stored in large quantities, the exact required temperatures and degrees of humidity for the various vegetables have to be observed.

In general, store root vegetables at a temperature somewhat below 50° F. but not low enough to cause freezing, and in a slightly humid atmosphere. Ventilated barrels, boxes, loosely woven bags, or crates, are the best containers for root vegetables; they may also be piled up along the wall. Potatoes and celery can be stored like root vegetables, but potatoes should be protected from light. Lay late cabbage in rows on shelves, preferably in an outdoor storage cellar. Onions require a somewhat dryer place than root vegetables to prevent them from sprouting. Store pumpkins and squash in rows on shelves in a dry place. Sweet potatoes can be stored like Irish potatoes; they are, however, more perishable and must be handled carefully to prevent bruises and mold.

CANNED VEGETABLES: They should be stored in a cool, dry place; if in glass jars, keep them in a dark place to protect them from exposure to light.

FROZEN VEGETABLES: These must be kept in the freezer or the freezing unit of the refrigerator, and in the latter, not too long. Do not attempt to refreeze thawed vegetables.

DRIED AND DEHYDRATED VEGETABLES: They will keep well in any cool and dry place. If removed from the original package, store in tightly covered containers.

LEFTOVER VEGETABLES: Place in not too large containers, cool quickly; cover tightly; keep in refrigerator, and use up as soon as possible. Never store raw leafy salads when mixed with dressing. Canned food can safely be left in the cans after they have been opened, provided they are tightly covered and kept in the refrigerator. Otherwise, it has to be treated like any other perishable food.

VEGETABLE STOCK: All liquid that is drained off cooked vegetables, or vegetable stock, must be kept in the refrigerator, tightly covered. Like any other cooked food, cool before storing. Do not remove fat, if present, until liquid is to be used, as it protects the stock against spoilage.

Cooking Guide

THIS IS a cookbook within a cookbook. It contains all the essential facts for the various ways of cooking and serving each vegetable. It gives all step-by-step directions, so that even the inexperienced cook can follow with ease.

Cooking time varies with the method of cooking and with a vegetable's freshness, size and quantity. For this reason, cooking time indicates only the range between the lower and upper limits. The charts give cooking time for steaming (other than in the pressure cooker) and gentle boiling, based on *quantities for four average servings*.

As has been pointed out elsewhere in this book, steaming is the method of choice in preparing fresh vegetables. This method is described in detail here, whereas cooking in water, which varies with each vegetable, is described in detail in the chart which follows. A very few vegetables can be neither boiled nor steamed, and directions will be found under the vegetables in question.

Steaming can be done either in a steamer or in a pressure cooker. When using the pressure cooker, follow directions and cooking time which apply to the pressure cooker used. As for steamers, there are several varieties on the market, but the ingenious homemaker can, without difficulty, devise her own steamer or steamers. Since the purpose of steaming is to cook vegetables by contact with steam rather than with water, the boiling water should never touch the vegetables, and the pots must always be tightly covered. The more boiling water and the more steam formed, the better for the vegetable. Keep water at a constant boil and do not uncover the vegetable until cooking time has elapsed.

Such things as wire frying basket, colanders, cloth bags or perforated inset pans can all be used for steaming, provided they fit into the pot without falling into the water. If none of these is available, a strong square of cloth will serve the purpose. Knot each of the four corners so that the cloth fits over the pot, but with enough give to provide room for the vegetable. To make assurance doubly sure, slip a piece of wood through one of the knots.

In general, use the smallest possible amount of water when vegetables are to be water-cooked. Use pots with tightly fitting lids, and neither so small as to overcrowd nor so large as to need much water. With a few exceptions, add vegetables to briskly boiling water, let come to a boil, and turn flame low enough to simmer (which is cooking just below boiling point).

As water-cooking dissolves the water-soluble nutrients in vegetables, a great loss of food value occurs when water in which vegetables have been cooked is allowed to go down the kitchen drain. Vegetable "water" can be used for soups, stews and sauces.

Leafy vegetables, such as spinach, chard and "tops," need no additional water, the water adhering to the leaves after washing being sufficient, if the vegetable is cooked over a low flame and in a tightly covered pot. Cucumbers and tomatoes, which are watery, need the addition of only a little water. Other vegetables need just enough water to barely cover, the quantity depending on kind of vegetable and size of pot; root vegetables must be covered with water; while beets, corn, potatoes, and turnips must be amply covered with water.

Cook vegetables in their skins and whole, whenever possible. Needless to say, if peel you must, peel paperthin.

Strong-flavored vegetables, such as Brussels sprouts, cabbage, cauliflower and kale, should either be blanched or be allowed to stand in slightly salted, cold water for about thirty minutes before cooking.

Some recipes call for parboiling in order to shorten the time of baking or scalloping, and for basting during the baking.

TO BLANCH: Cover with boiling salted water and let stand for about five minutes. Use fresh water for cooking.

TO PARBOIL: Cook vegetables for five to ten minutes and drain.

TO BASTE: Moisten with small quantities of liquid to prevent food from drying while baking or broiling.

Wash all vegetables immediately before cooking, even those that have been washed before storing. Do not overcook vegetables: cook only *until tender*. Taste and texture are the way to judge tenderness. These vary with the vegetable: some are soft, others firm. Such vegetables as beets, potatoes, carrots and asparagus are tender when they admit a fork easily; others, such as cauliflower and broccoli, are tender when soft enough to be crushed without difficulty between the fingers; snap beans, Brussels sprouts, celery, cabbage, and peas are best tested by tasting. Overcooked vegetables may be too soft, flabby, mealy or mushy, some even tough, and many change color.

Do not oversalt vegetables during cooking. It is better to use only a little salt and add salt "to taste" when vegetable is tender or before serving. Leafy vegetables and those with a sweet taste need less salt than white, strong-flavored or tough vegetables. A very few should be cooked without any salt. In many cases the salt should be added only after the vegetable has been cooking for a few minutes, but some vegetables should be dropped into boiling water to which the salt has already been added.

The quantity of salt depends on the texture and kind of vegetable, some needing slightly salted, others salted boiling water. For "slightly salted," add ¼ teaspoon salt per pound of vegetable to the cooking water; for "salted," add ½ teaspoon salt per pound of vegetable to the cooking water.

The simplest way to serve cooked vegetables is either "buttered" or creamed. Besides the addition of seasoning and some form of fat or a cream or white sauce to vegetables, they can also be scalloped or fried; some vegetables can be glazed, many can be served au gratin, some as croquettes and fritters, and a few lend themselves to stuffing or mashing.

Such vegetables as asparagus, broccoli, lima and snap beans, Brussel sprouts, cabbage, cauliflower, celery, corn, eggplant, leeks, mushrooms, onions, peas, potatoes, spinach and turnip greens can be creamed.

All leftover vegetables, as well as all fresh vegetables, can be scalloped.

In addition to onions and mushrooms, watery vegetables, such as cucumbers, tomatoes and some varieties of squash, can be panned.

TO CREAM: Add 1 cup medium white sauce to 3 to 4 cups cooked vegetables. Mix well and heat thoroughly in top of a double boiler.

To Scallop: Place 3 cups sliced or diced cooked vegetables in layers in a well-greased baking dish; pour white sauce or milk over each layer, dot with fat, and bake, uncovered, in a moderate oven for about 20 minutes. Or cut raw vegetables into bite size (3 cups), place in baking dish, dredge with 1 to 2 tablespoons flour, and pour 2 tablespoons melted fat and 1 cup milk over vegetables. Bake, uncovered, in a slow oven until tender.

Au Gratin: Prepare as for scalloping. Place cooked vegetables in a deep or shallow well-greased baking dish. Cover with grated cheese, dot with fat, and brown in a moderate oven for 10 to 25 minutes. This can also be done under the broiler if the vegetable is still hot.

To Glaze: Cook sugar in a small quantity of water until syrupy, add fat and blend well, add vegetable, and cook for a few minutes. Stir frequently to prevent scorching. Carrots, beets and onions lend themselves to glazing.

To Pan: Heat a small amount of fat, preferably in a heavy skillet, add chopped or cut-up vegetable, and cook over a very low flame. An asbestos mat will prevent scorching.

To Purée: Press cooked vegetables through a sieve or put through a food mill.

To Fry in Deep Fat: All oils except olive oil and all solid fats except butter can be used. Kettle should be two-thirds full of fat. Fry only small quantities of food at a time. If a frying basket is used, put in only enough of the vegetable to cover its bottom, and shake the basket lightly during frying. Fry until light brown and drain on soft unglazed paper.

The temperature of the hot fat for deep-fat frying depends on the vegetable to be fried, and care must be taken to keep it constant.

Fritters and croquettes are usually fried in deep fat, and many vegetables, both raw and cooked, can also be prepared in this way. With the exception of potatoes and onions, vegetables must be coated with batter before being fried in deep fat.

TO MAKE FRITTERS: Dip well-drained or dried vegetables in batter until well coated, lift out with fork and lower carefully into hot fat. Fry until brown, remove with skimmer, or lift out frying basket, and drain on paper.

TO MAKE CROQUETTES: Chop or purée 2 cups cooked vegetables and mix with 1 cup thick white sauce. Shape into croquettes of uniform size. Dip into egg, then into crumbs, and fry in deep hot fat until golden brown. Drain on paper.

DROP BATTER
1 egg
2 tablesps. milk
Salt, to taste
4 to 5 tablesps. flour

Beat egg, add milk, salt, and enough flour to make a thin batter.

FRENCH PANCAKE BATTER
1 cup milk
1 egg
Salt, to taste
½ cup flour

Mix ½ cup milk with egg and salt and beat well with rotary beater. Add flour and stir until smooth. Add remaining milk and blend well. Avoid beating. Use additional milk if batter is too thick, additional flour if batter is too thin.

COOKING CHART FOR FRESH VEGETABLES

	Cooking Time (in Minutes)	
	Steaming	*"Boiling"*

Artichokes

   French or Globe

    Cut off stem; remove loose outer leaves; snip off sharp tips of leaves with scissors; place in saucepan just large enough to hold the artichokes comfortably; cover with boiling water, add 1 teaspoon each of salt and lemon juice or vinegar to each quart of water; cover and cook briskly until tender. When outer leaves pull off easily, artichokes are tender. Remove from water, and turn upside down on a plate to drain. **[Do not steam | 25 to 35]**

    The spiny choke which covers the heart is inedible; it can be scooped out with the handle of a spoon before serving or removed with a knife when the leaves have been eaten.

    Serve with melted butter, French dressing, or mayonnaise thinned with lemon juice, in a separate dish. Do not pour dressing over artichokes.

   Jerusalem

    Scrape and put immediately into cold water, to which some vinegar has been added, to prevent artichokes from darkening. Drain, cover with boiling water, add ½ teaspoon salt, and cook, covered, until tender. Overcooking toughens this vegetable. **[Do not steam | 20 to 30]**

    Serve whole or diced, with butter and seasoning.

Asparagus

    Snap or cut off tough ends; lightly peel or scrape lower portion of stalk if asparagus is thick; tie in a bundle with cord. **[15 to 30 | 15 to 20]**

	Cooking Time (in Minutes
	Steaming	"Boiling"

Asparagus—continued

To steam: Stand upright in about 3 inches of boiling, slightly salted water in lower part of double boiler or in a deep pot, cover with top of double boiler or lid, and cook until tender. *To boil:* Cover with boiling water, add ½ teaspoon salt, and cook, covered, until tender. Drain.

Serve with melted butter and lemon juice, hot mayonnaise, or Hollandaise.

Avocados   To be served raw

Chill before using; peel, cut in half, slice, or cube.

Beans, Lima, Fava, and Soybeans (Fresh Green)

Shell beans, barely cover with boiling water, simmer, covered, for 5 minutes, add 1 teaspoon salt, and continue simmering until tender. Drain, if necessary.   25 to 40   20 to 35

Serve with melted butter and seasoning.

Snap (String)

Remove ends and strings, if any. If beans are large, cut crosswise in 2-inch pieces or in thin strips lengthwise. Add a small amount (about 3 cups) of boiling water (quantity depends on size and shape of pot), and simmer, covered, until tender; drain.   20 to 35   15 to 30

Serve with butter, seasoning and chopped parsley.

Wax (Yellow)

Prepare like snap beans, add 1 medium-sized tart apple, thinly pared, cored, and sliced. Cook like snap beans; drain.   25 to 35   20 to 30

Serve with butter, chopped parsley, chives or dill, and seasoning.

	Cooking Time (in Minutes)	
	Steaming	"Boiling"

Beets, Mature

Leave roots and 2 inches of stem on beets. Cover amply with cold, slightly salted water, bring to quick boil, then simmer, covered, until tender. Rinse in cold water to slip off skins.

Serve sliced or cubed, with butter, lemon juice, salt and sugar.   45 to 60   30 to 60

Young Beets

Scrape if desired, shred on a medium shredder, add just enough cold water to prevent scorching, a pinch of salt, and cook, covered, over a low flame; drain, if necessary.

Serve with butter, sugar and a very little salt.   8 to 10   5 to 8

Broccoli

Remove leaves and 1 or 2 inches of stems; let stand in cold salted water for 15 to 20 minutes; rinse. Slit stalks part of the way up; cover with boiling salted water, and cook, covered, until tender.

Serve like asparagus.   20 to 30   15 to 25

Brussels Sprouts

Blanch, or soak in cold salted water for 30 minutes; rinse. Cover with boiling water, add ½ teaspoon salt, and cook, covered, until tender. Do not overcook. Drain.

Serve with butter and seasoning.   20 to 25   15 to 20

Cabbage (All Varieties)

Remove outside leaves, blanch and shred, slice thin, or cut in wedges, depending on variety of cabbage and personal preference. Add a small amount (2 to 3 cups) of boiling water (quantity depends on size and shape of pot), and ½ teaspoon salt; simmer, covered, until tender, turning once or twice during cooking; drain.

Serve with butter, salt and pepper.   10 to 20   8 to 15

	Cooking Time (in Minutes)	
	Steaming	"Boiling"

Carrots

Scrape or peel very thin; leave small carrots whole; slice or cut larger carrots. Add a small amount (1 ½ to 2 cups) of boiling water (quantity depends on size and shape of pot), simmer, covered, for 5 minutes, add ¼ teaspoon salt, and continue simmering until tender. Drain, if necessary. — **20 to 30** | **15 to 25**

Serve with butter, salt and chopped parsley or anise or glaze.

Cauliflower

Blanch, or let stand (head down) in cold, salted water for 30 minutes; rinse. Cover (head up) with boiling water, add 1 teaspoon salt and 1 teaspoon lemon juice or vinegar, and simmer, covered, until tender. Cauliflower is tender when a small floweret crushes easily between fingers. Drain. — **25 to 30** | **20 to 30**

Overcooking discolors cauliflower.

Cooking time is shortened by 5 to 10 minutes if cauliflower is broken into flowerets before cooking.

Serve covered with buttered bread or cracker crumbs, cream or cheese sauce, or au gratin.

Celeriac

See Celery Knob.

Celery, Green or White

Take stalks apart, leaving hearts whole; remove coarse strings; do not remove leaves; cut into 2-inch pieces. Add boiling water to barely cover, simmer, covered, for 5 minutes, add ½ teaspoon salt, and continue simmering until tender. — **20 to 30** | **10 to 25**

Celery can also be panned.

Serve with tomato or cheese sauce.

Cooking Time
(*in Minutes*)

	Steaming	"Boiling"

Knob
  Pare or scrape; leave whole, cube or slice.
Cover with slightly salted boiling water, and
simmer, covered, until tender. Slice or cube
if cooked whole.
  Serve with lemon butter and seasoning; or
with white or cheese sauce.

Chard, Swiss
  Prepare and cook like spinach. Stems, when
very large, may be cooked separately and
served like asparagus.   18 to 20   10 to 15

Chayotes
  Do not pare; cook whole or sliced. Cover with
boiling salted water and simmer, covered, until
tender. Drain.   20 to 35   20 to 30
  Serve with butter, salt and pepper.

Chestnuts
  Shell before cooking. To shell, cut a half-inch
slit on flat side, cover with boiling water, and   Do not   20 to 25
soak for 3 to 5 minutes. Remove one at a time   steam
from water and peel off brown skin with sharp
knife.
  Cover with boiling water, add ½ teaspoon
salt, and simmer, covered, until tender. If chestnuts are to be served pureed, press through
sieve while chestnuts are very hot.
  Serve with butter, salt and pepper; or
creamed, puréed, or panned.

Chicory
  See Endive, French.

Collards
  Prepare and cook like spinach.   25 to 30   15 to 20
  Serve with butter and seasoning.

Cooking Time
(in Minutes)

	Steaming	"Boiling"
Corn, Sweet Remove husks and silk, plunge into boiling water to amply cover, and simmer, covered, until tender. Add 1 teaspoon sugar to cooking water if a very sweet taste is desired. Serve with butter and salt on the side.	10 to 20	6 to 10
Cucumbers Used mainly raw in salads. Do not peel if cucumber is not bitter; quarter, or cut into thick slices, add enough water (about 1 ½ cups) to prevent scorching (quantity depends on size and shape of pot) and ½ teaspoon salt. Cook, covered, over a low flame until tender. Serve with sour cream or lemon butter.	15 to 20	10 to 15
Dandelion Greens Can be eaten raw or prepared like spinach.	15 to 20	10 to 15
Dasheens Cook in skins; do not scrape; prepare like potatoes, but do not mash.	20 to 35	20 to 30
Eggplant Do not peel; cube or cut into fingerthick slices and sprinkle with lemon juice to prevent darkening; add enough boiling water to barely cover, ½ teaspoon salt, and simmer, covered, until tender. Drain, if necessary. Eggplant can also be panned. Serve with butter, chopped parsley, and seasoning, or with tomato sauce.	Do not steam	10 to 15
Endive, Curly Used mainly raw in salads. Remove wilted and coarse leaves; cook and serve like romaine.	20 to 25	15 to 20

Cooking Time
(in Minutes)

	Steaming	"Boiling"
Endive, French (Blanched or Witloof Chicory) Used mainly raw in salads. Cook and serve like romaine.	25 to 30	20 to 25
Escarole Used mainly raw in salads. Cook and serve like romaine.	15 to 20	10 to 15
Fennel (Finochio) Cut off leafy part and chop; cut heart into halves or quarters. Cover both with boiling water, add ½ teaspoon salt, and simmer, covered, until tender. Drain, if necessary. Serve with butter, salt and pepper, or with tomato sauce.	15 to 20	10 to 15
"Greens" Both wild greens and the tops of beets and turnips. Prepare like spinach or use in salads.	15 to 25	10 to 20
Kale Remove heavy stems and blanch; leave whole or cut into pieces. Add enough water to barely cover, ½ teaspoon salt, and simmer, covered, until tender, turning once or twice during cooking. Chop fine. Serve with butter, and pepper and salt; or with white sauce, or sour cream.	25 to 30	20 to 25
Knob Celery See Celery Knob.		
Kohlrabi Cook whole unpeeled, or peel thinly, and quarter or slice. Chop smallest inner leaves, and cook with kohlrabi. Add enough water to barely cover, ½ teaspoon salt, and simmer, covered, until tender. Drain, if necessary. Peel and slice, if cooked unpeeled. Serve with butter, salt and pepper; or with sour cream, or white sauce.	25 to 35	25 to 30

Cooking Time
(in Minutes)

	Steaming	"Boiling"
Leeks	15 to 20	10 to 15

Leeks
  Trim off root ends and all faded parts of leaves. Let stand in cold salted water for 30 minutes; rinse. Leave whole or cut into 3-inch lengths. Split outer layers of bulb and separate green leaves for better washing. Barely cover with boiling water, add a pinch of salt, and simmer, covered, until tender. Drain.
  Serve with butter, salt, pepper or nutmeg; or sprinkled with grated cheese, or covered with cheese sauce.

Lettuce
  Used mainly raw in salads.
  Cook and serve like spinach.

	8 to 15	5 to 10

Mushrooms   Best when panned
  Do not peel. Remove stems, and cut off stem ends; if mushrooms are small, leave whole; otherwise, slice or quarter. Pan over a very low flame in melted butter or other fat together with finely chopped parsley. Do not overcook, as mushrooms become tough and shriveled.
  Serve seasoned with salt and pepper; or in sour cream or white sauce.

Okra (Gumbo)   15 to 25   10 to 25
  Cut off stems, slice in ½-inch pieces, cover with slightly salted boiling water, and simmer, covered, until tender. If okra shows tough strings when being sliced, it can be used only in soup, not as a vegetable. Drain, if necessary; add a dash of vinegar and sprinkle with salt.
  Serve plain, or with cheese sauce or sour cream.

Cooking Time
(in Minutes)

	Steaming	"Boiling"

Onions, Dry

Remove dry outer skins. Amply cover with slightly salted boiling water and simmer, covered, until tender. Drain, if necessary, and quarter if onion is large.

Serve with butter and salt; or with white sauce.

	Steaming	"Boiling"
Onions, Dry	Do not steam	20 to 30

  Green

  See Scallions.

Oysterplant

  See Salsify.

Parsnips

Cook whole unpeeled, or peeled and sliced into rounds. Cover with slightly salted, boiling water, and simmer, covered, until tender. Drain, and remove skins, if necessary; slice, if whole.

Serve sprinkled with grated cheese; or with cheese sauce.

| Parsnips | 30 to 40 | 20 to 30 |

Peas

Shell, add a small amount (about 2 cups) of boiling water (quantity depends on size and shape of pot), ½ teaspoon sugar, and 1 or 2 lettuce leaves, which keep peas from losing color and shrinking. Simmer, covered, until tender. Drain if necessary.

Serve with butter, salt and chopped parsley; or in white sauce.

| Peas | 20 to 30 | 10 to 20 |

Peppers, Green

To prepare peppers for stuffing or baking, cut off stem end, remove seeds, and parboil. Drain.

| Peppers, Green | Do not steam | 5 to 10 |

Potatoes, White (Irish)

Remove eyes and blemishes, and rootlets, if any. Amply cover with cold, slightly salted water and cook, covered, until tender. Peel; leave whole, or slice or cube.

| Potatoes, White (Irish) | 25 to 35 | 20 to 30 |

Cooking Time
(in Minutes)

	Steaming	"Boiling"

Potatoes, White (Irish) — *continued*

Serve with butter and seasoning; or creamed, scalloped, or mashed.

For mashed potatoes add ¼ cup of hot milk, butter and seasoning, and beat until light and fluffy. For baking choose even-sized, well-shaped potatoes, scrub well, dry, rub skins lightly with fat and bake in a moderate oven for 40 to 50 minutes. Potatoes are done when they yield easily to pressure of fingers.

For French-fried potatoes cut peeled potatoes into long strips ¼- to ½-inch thick. Soak 1 hour in cold water to cover; drain and dry between towels. Fry a few strips at a time in hot deep fat until delicately brown. Shake frying basket during frying. Drain on paper and sprinkle with salt. (Use 1 medium potato per serving.)

Sweet and Yams — Steaming 25 to 30 — "Boiling" 20 to 30

Cover with slightly salted, boiling water, and cook, covered, until tender. Drain, and peel.

Serve with butter; or creamed or mashed.

For baking, dry after washing, bake in a moderate oven until tender (20 to 30 minutes, depending on size).

Radishes, Red or White — Steaming: Do not steam — "Boiling" 15 to 20

Mainly eaten raw.

Remove outer leaves and roots. Cut larger radishes in half, leave small ones whole. Barely cover with cold water, add chopped inner leaves and ¼ teaspoon salt. Simmer, covered, until tender.

Serve sprinkled with chopped chives or grated cheese; or in white sauce or sour cream.

	Steaming	"Boiling"
Romaine (Lettuce)	15 to 20	10 to 15

Romaine (Lettuce)
Take apart and remove wilted leaves. Leave small leaves whole, cut larger ones in half. Add enough water (about 1 ½ to 2 cups) to barely cover (quantity depends on size and shape of pot), ¼ teaspoon salt, and simmer, covered, until tender. Drain, if necessary.
Serve like spinach.

Rutabagas
See Turnips, Yellow.

Salsify (Oysterplant)
Scrape and put in cold water to which 1 tablespoon vinegar for each quart of water has been added, to prevent salsify from darkening. Leave whole or cut into 2-inch pieces; drop into slightly salted, boiling water to cover, and simmer, covered, until tender. Drain, if necessary.

(Salsify) — Steaming: Do not steam — "Boiling": 20 to 45

Serve with butter and seasoning; or in sour cream or cheese sauce.
For frying, parboil, drain well, dredge in flour, and fry in hot fat until crisp.

Scallions (Green Onions)   Steaming: 10 to 20 — "Boiling": 8 to 15
Cook and serve like leeks; or pan.

Soybeans, Fresh Green
See Beans.

Soybean Sprouts
Barely cover with slightly salted, boiling water, and simmer, covered, until tender. Drain; the loose bean skins need not be discarded.

(Soybean Sprouts) — Steaming: Do not steam — "Boiling": 10 to 12

Serve with a little fat, salt and pepper.

	Cooking Time (in Minutes)	
	Steaming	*"Boiling"*

To pan, heat 1 to 2 tablespoons fat, add sprouts and 1 to 2 tablespoons hot water, and cook for 10 minutes stirring frequently. Be careful not to crush the sprouts. Season with salt.

Spinach

Do not drain after washing, as the water which clings to leaves after washing is sufficient for cooking. Cook covered for 5 minutes over a very low flame, add ¼ teaspoon salt, and simmer, covered, until tender. Turn once during cooking. Drain and chop fine.   *(Steaming: 10 to 15 — "Boiling": 8 to 10)*

Serve with butter and seasoning; or with white sauce or sour cream.

Squash, Acorn (Des Moines)

Split in half lengthwise, scoop out seeds and stringy portions, place butter or vegetable shortening, brown sugar, salt and pepper in centers. Bake in shallow baking dish in about ½ inch of water, in a moderate oven until tender (30 to 45 minutes).   *(To be baked)*

Hubbard (Winter)

Split open, remove seeds and stringy portions; pare, cut in 2-inch pieces, drop into slightly salted, boiling water, add 1 teaspoon vinegar, and simmer, covered, until tender; drain.   *(Steaming: 20 to 30 — "Boiling": 20 to 25)*

Serve mashed or as is, with butter and seasoning.

Hubbard squash is frequently baked: split in half, remove seeds and stringy portions, fill center with milk, add brown sugar, salt, pepper, and nutmeg. Set into a baking dish in about 1 inch of water, and bake in a moderate oven until tender (45 to 60 minutes). Add more water during baking, if necessary.

Vegetable Marrow

Cut into 4-inch slices; cook and serve like summer squash.   *(Steaming: 20 to 30 — "Boiling": 15 to 20)*

Cooking Time
(in Minutes)

	Steaming	"Boiling"

Yellow (Summer)

Scrub, remove ends and blemishes, and peel, | 20 to 30 | 15 to 25
if skin is tough. Slide or cube, and remove
stringy or spongy parts, if any. Add enough
(about 1 ½ cups) boiling water to prevent
scorching (quantity depends on size and shape
of pot), a pinch of salt, and simmer, covered,
until tender. Drain if necessary.

Serve with butter, salt and pepper.

Zucchini (Italian Squash)

Cut off stems and remove blemishes. Slice | 20 to 25 | 15 to 18
crosswise in ¾-inch slices, cover with boiling
water, add a pinch of salt, and simmer, covered,
until tender.

Serve with butter and seasoning.

This vegetable is often panned; slice very
thin, pan in hot fat, covered, for 10 to 15
minutes, and season with salt and marjoram or
pepper.

Sweet Potatoes

See Potatoes, Sweet.

Swiss Chard

See Chard, Swiss.

Tomatoes

Remove blemishes and blossom ends; leave | 10 to 15 | 5 to 15
whole, if to be steamed. For stewing, quarter
or cut in pieces, add 1 or 2 tablespoons water
if cooked over direct flame; no water if cooked
in top of double boiler; season with salt, sugar
and a bit of onion, or onion juice, and simmer,
covered, until tender.

Serve with butter and chopped parsley.

Tomatoes lend themselves to broiling: cut
in half, place in shallow baking dish, dot with
butter or vegetable shortening, season with salt,
and sprinkle with a few bread-crumbs, or grated
cheese, if desired; place under medium broiler
heat, and broil until tender (10 to 15 minutes).

Vegetable Marrow

See Squash.

Cooking Time
(in Minutes)

	Steaming	"Boiling"
Turnips, White		
Pare, and cube or slice; cover with large amount of boiling water, to which 1 teaspoon of sugar has been added for each quart of water, and simmer, covered, until tender. Do not add salt during cooking. Drain.	20 to 35	15 to 30
Serve with salt and black pepper or marjoram; or in lemon sauce or hot mayonnaise.		
Yellow (Rutabagas)		
Prepare and cook like white turnips. When tender, drain, mash, and add butter and seasoning.	20 to 40	15 to 35
Water Cress		
Used mainly raw in salads.		
Yams		
See Potatoes, Sweet.		
Zucchini		
See Squash.		

DRIED VEGETABLES (LEGUMES)

Pick over, and wash dried peas, beans and lentils in several waters. One cup of dried vegetables makes 3 to 4 cups cooked. Cover with 4 to 5 cups of cold water for each cup of legume used. Soak for at least 12 hours, preferably overnight. Taste soaking water before putting on to cook; if bitter, discard, and cover amply with fresh cold water. Bring to a boil, then simmer, covered, until tender, adding warm water during cooking, if needed. Legumes are tender when soft enough to crush easily between fingers.

Cooking time varies with kind, quantity, and quality of vegetable, and ranges from 1 ¾ to 4 hours. There are some tenderized beans and peas on the market which do not need as much time; follow package directions.

Serve with salt and pepper, either plain or pureed (which must be done while legumes are still hot), or with butter or a well-seasoned sauce.

The different varieties of dried peas and beans now on the market are:

Peas, yellow and green, whole or split.

Red and white beans, black turtle beans, lima, yellow, marrow and pea beans.

Lentils.

Soybeans.

CANNED VEGETABLES

These need only be heated, which is most easily done by draining off the liquid and heating the vegetable in a double boiler. Another method in common use is to boil the liquid in a saucepan until it is reduced to about half, add the vegetable, and heat quickly.

FROZEN VEGETABLES

Since they are harvested at their peak of quality and flavor, and instantly quick frozen, the nutritional value of frozen is almost twin to garden-fresh vegetables.

As quick freezing softens the fiber, the cooking time of frozen vegetables is shorter than of fresh. Do not thaw before cooking, but drop while still frozen into rapidly boiling water; then simmer according to package directions.

Seasoning Guide

PROPERLY PREPARED, vegetables need little seasoning, yet fragrant herbs and spices can add zest and variety to the simplest dish. Since herbs and spices have a distinct flavor of their own (and in a few cases pungent), it is better to err by using them too sparingly than too liberally, particularly if you are a novice in the art of seasoning. Some seasonings have an affinity for each other; others, when combined, wage war. While personal taste must decide both kind and quantity used, the following guide suggests which seasoning will go well with each vegetable. These suggestions, however, do not indicate any combinations.

ARTICHOKES, FRENCH OR GLOBE: Celery Salt, Garlic, Paprika, Parsley, Red Pepper, Sage, Savory.
— JERUSALEM: Bay Leaf, Chili Powder, Marjoram, Nutmeg, Paprika, Red Pepper.

ASPARAGUS: Celery Salt, Marjoram, White Pepper.
ASPARAGUS SOUP: Celery Salt, Chervil, Chives, Parsley, Tarragon.

Beans, Lima or Soybeans (Fresh): Marjoram, Paprika, Red Pepper, Rosemary.
 Bean Soup: Borage, Chives, Dill.
— **Snap (String) or Wax:** Borage, Black Pepper, Celery Salt, Marjoram.

Beets: Bay Leaf, Chervil, Coriander, Dill, Mustard Seeds, Onion Powder, Sage, Tarragon.
 Beet Salad: Chervil, Horseradish, Parsley, Savory, Tarragon.

Broccoli: Borage, Celery Salt, Marjoram, Paprika, Red Pepper, Savory, White Pepper.

Brussels Sprouts: Celery Salt, Coriander, Garlic, Mace, Nutmeg, Paprika, Thyme.

Cabbage, Green and White: Black Pepper, Caraway Seeds, Paprika, Sage.
 Cole Slaw: Basil (Sweet), Chives, Marjoram, Thyme.
— **Red:** Caraway Seeds, Celery Salt, Ginger, Sage, Savory.
— **Cabbage Salad:** Basil (Sweet), Borage, Chives, Garlic, Marjoram.

Carrots: Anise Seeds, Celery Salt, Mace, Onion Juice, Sage.
 Carrot Salad: Basil, Chives, Parsley, Tarragon.

Cauliflower: Basil, Coriander, Dry Mustard, Mace, Nutmeg, Savory, White Pepper.
 Cauliflower Salad: Basil, Chives, Onion Juice.

Celery, Green and White: Chervil, Horseradish, Paprika, Parsley.
— **Knob:** Marjoram, Paprika, Parsley, Red Pepper.

CELERY SALAD: Chervil, Horseradish, Marjoram, Paprika, Parsley.

CHARD, SWISS: Allspice, Celery Salt, Chili Powder, Curry, Paprika, Red Pepper, Savory.

CUCUMBERS: Black Pepper, Chervil, Dill, Marjoram, Paprika, Parsley.
CUCUMBER SALAD: Borage, Chives, Sage.

EGGPLANT: Basil, Celery Salt, Chervil, Dill, Garlic, Marjoram, Paprika, Parsley, Tarragon.

FENNEL: Borage, Chives, Parsley.

KALE: Black Pepper, Horseradish, Marjoram, Nutmeg, Olives.

KOHLRABI: Marjoram, Nutmeg, Paprika, Red Pepper.

LEEKS: Celery Salt.

LETTUCE: Basil, Borage, Cayenne Pepper, Celery, Chervil, Coriander, Dill, Mace, Marjoram, Red Pepper, Rosemary, Sage, Savory, Tarragon, Thyme.

MUSHROOMS: Celery Salt, Chives, Marjoram, Mint, Parsley, Red Pepper, White Pepper.

PARSNIPS: Black Pepper, Dill, Marjoram.

PEAS: Rosemary, Sage, Thyme.
PEA SOUP: Marjoram, Red Pepper, Savory.

POTATOES, WHITE (IRISH):Bay Leaf, Caraway Seeds, Celery Salt, Dill, Marjoram, Mint, Red Pepper, White Pepper.

POTATO SOUP: Marjoram, Tarragon.

POTATO SALAD: Dry Mustard, Onion Juice, White Pepper.

SWEET AND YAMS: Celery Salt, Coriander, Ginger, Mace, Thyme.

SALSIFY (OYSTERPLANT): Borage, Chives, Marjoram, Onion Juice, Paprika, Red Pepper, Savory.

SAUERKRAUT: Caraway Seeds, Juniper Berries, Paprika, White Pepper.

SPINACH: Celery Salt, Curry, Ginger (a pinch), Marjoram, Savory, Sweet Basil, Thyme.

SQUASH (ALL VARIETIES): Bay Leaf, Curry, Paprika, Parsley, Red Pepper.

TOMATOES: Bay Leaf, Chervil, Chives, Fennel, Garlic, Paprika, Parsley, Red Pepper, Sweet Basil, Tarragon, Water Cress.

TURNIPS, WHITE AND YELLOW: Black Pepper, Caraway Seeds, Celery Salt, Curry, Dill, Paprika.

PART THREE

Recipes
"Cooked To Your Taste"

Introduction

ALL RECIPES in the pages to follow have an element
of novelty about them and are desirable from the point
of view of good nutrition. The classic ways of cooking
vegetables attractively have been condensed in the
easy-to-follow "Cooking Guide."

All recipes have stood the test of time, for the author
has repeatedly used them in her own home. And
although there are many recipes for main-dish vegetables, none of them are difficult or time-consuming.

Since seasoning is very much a matter of personal
taste, the recipes give it "to taste," so that you may
use any or all and as much or as little as suits your
fancy. For salt, any salt (including sea salt, vegetized
salt or sodium-free substitute) may be used, if desired.

Whenever a recipe mentions a sauce, find the recipe
under "Sauces and Salad Dressings." Fragrantly-
seasoned sauces complement the blander vegetables.

A word about fats: whenever a recipe calls for oil
or butter, oil being the first mentioned, the dish is
best prepared with oil. A choice has been offered, however, since there are strong personal preferences when
it comes to fat. But when butter is used in such recipes,
a little more is needed than called for in the recipe;
for example, 3 tablespoons oil or butter — 3 ½ tablespoons butter.

79

As for cream, all recipes calling for cream assume the use of light cream. In many cases there is no perceptible difference whether sour cream or plain yogurt is used, but in the few cases where such a substitution is not possible, the recipe calls only for cream.

Few dishes improve by standing, and vegetable dishes especially should be served as soon as they are ready. Such dishes as contain stiffly beaten egg whites must be served immediately and are so indicated in the recipes.

Quantities in all recipes have been figured on the basis of *four generous servings;* this means that when a dish is-not the main course of the meal, it can be made to serve five to six.

TABLE OF MEASURES AND TEMPERATURES

MEASUREMENTS (LEVEL)

3 teaspoons — 1 tablespoon
16 tablespoons — 1 cup
2 cups — 1 pint
2 pints — 1 quart
4 quarts — 1 gallon

TEMPERATURES

Oven Temperatures (Preheat Oven, if necessary)

Moderately slow oven	325° F.
Moderate oven	350° F.
Moderately hot oven	375° F.
Hot oven	400° F.

Deep-Fat Frying (at Sea Level)

Kind of food	Temperature	Test if no thermometer is available: time required to brown one-inch cube of bread in hot fat	Frying Time (Minutes)
Raw, dry foods and fritters	365 to 370° F.	60 seconds	3 to 5
Potatoes (chips and French Fried)	380 to 395°F.	40 to 45 seconds	4 to 8
Cooked, dry foods and croquettes	385 to 390° F.	40 seconds	1 to 2

ABBREVIATIONS

Tablesp., tablesps., teasp. and teasps. stand, of course, for tablespoon, tablespoons, teaspoon and teaspoons.

Fresh Vegetables

ITALIAN-STYLE ARTICHOKES

4 medium artichokes
    (French or globe)
2 cloves garlic
1 teasp. chopped parsley
Salt, to taste

Cayenne pepper, if desired
6 tablesps. oil, preferably
    olive oil
Water, as needed

1. Wash artichokes carefully, cut off stems, and snip off the sharp tips of leaves with scissors. Loosen leaves slightly.

2. Crush garlic and mix with chopped parsley, salt and a dash of cayenne pepper, and place the mixture between the loosened leaves of the artichokes. Put artichokes into a small top-of-the-stove baking dish, pour 1 to 1 ½ tablesps. oil over each artichoke. Pour 1 cup water in bottom of dish—not over the artichokes.

3. Cover and simmer over a low flame until leaves are tender. If additional water is needed, be careful not to pour it over the artichokes.

4. When artichokes are tender, turn them upside down and bake, uncovered, in a moderate oven for 5 minutes.

Serve either hot or cold.

STUFFED ARTICHOKES

4 medium globe artichokes
1 small onion or scallion
4 large mushrooms
2 to 3 tablesps. oil or butter
1 ½ tablesps. tomato paste

Salt and black pepper, to taste
3 tablesps. white wine
3 tablesps. water

1. Cook artichokes and drain.
2. Chop onion fine; slice mushrooms fine.
3. Pan onion and mushroom in hot fat for 5 minutes; add tomato paste, and cook over a low flame for another 5 minutes.
4. Pry leaves of artichokes apart gently; remove choke with handle of spoon, and season inside with salt and pepper.
5. Fill wells of artichokes with mixture, and tie in place with cord.
6. Place in baking dish, add wine and water, and cook for 10 minutes in a moderate oven, basting occasionally.
7. Remove cord and serve.

ARTICHOKE HEARTS

8 globe artichokes or frozen hearts
4 tablesps. light cream

2 tablesps. grated cheese
Salt, to taste
Dash of black pepper

1. If fresh artichokes are used, cook and drain; remove leaves and choke, and place hearts in a shallow baking dish.
2. Mix cream with cheese, salt and pepper, and spread over hearts.
3. Place under medium broiler for 15 minutes or until thoroughly heated and brown.
NOTE: Leaves can be served cold, with tart mayonnaise or French dressing.

ARTICHOKE HEARTS—TURKISH STYLE

1 teasp. chopped onion	taste
1 teasp. shredded carrot	8 artichoke hearts, cooked
1 teasp. sugar	fresh or frozen
5 tablesps. olive oil	2 cooked potatoes, sliced
5 tablesps. water	4 tablesps. cooked peas
Salt and black pepper, to	Chopped fennel or parsley

1. Mix onion, carrot and sugar with oil and water, and bring to a boil. Season with salt and pepper.

2. Add artichoke hearts, cover, and simmer for 10 minutes.

3. Mix with potatoes and peas and set aside to cool.

4. When cold, serve sprinkled with fennel or parsley.

JERUSALEM ARTICHOKES AU GRATIN

1 ½ pounds Jerusalem artichokes	Salt and nutmeg, to taste
	Oil
Lemon juice	Flour
6 to 8 black olives	1 teasp. chopped caraway
3 hard-cooked eggs	seeds
3 tablesps. tomato paste	½ cup sour cream or plain
4 tablesps. grated cheese	yogurt

1. Scrape and slice artichokes, and sprinkle immediately with lemon juice; pit and chop olives; slice eggs; mix tomato paste with cheese and seasoning.

2. Grease and flour baking dish, and place half of the artichokes in it.

3. Cover with egg slices and olives, sprinkle with caraway seeds, and spread with tomato mixture.

4. Cover with remaining artichokes; spread sour cream over it, and bake in a moderate oven, covered, for 25 to 30 minutes. Uncover and bake for 10 more minutes.

JERUSALEM ARTICHOKE FRITTERS

¼ cup flour	1 egg
Salt and white pepper, to taste	4 to 6 tablesps. bread or cracker crumbs
1 ½ pounds Jerusalem artichokes	Oil for deep frying

1. Sift flour together with salt and pepper.

2. Scrape artichokes, cut in ½-inch slices lengthwise and roll immediately in flour mixture.

3. Dip in beaten egg and roll in bread crumbs.

4. Deep-fry in hot oil until golden brown. Drain on paper.

5. Serve with a well-seasoned sauce.

STUFFED JERUSALEM ARTICHOKES— SPANISH STYLE

1 ½ pounds Jerusalem artichokes	olive oil
Lemon juice	Salt
½ pound fresh mushrooms or 1 cup canned	1 to 2 tablesps. cracker crumbs
1 fresh pimiento or 2 small canned	½ cup tomato juice or liquid from canned mushrooms
4 tablesps. oil, preferably	

1. Scrape and hollow out centers of artichokes (with a spoon or ball cutter). Rub immediately with lemon juice.

2. Chop pulp, mushrooms and pimiento, and pan in hot oil for 10 minutes. Season.

3. Mix with cracker crumbs and stuff artichoke shells.

4. Place in well-greased baking dish, pour liquid around them, cover, and bake in a moderate oven for 20 minutes. Uncover and bake for another 5 minutes.

JERUSALEM ARTICHOKES IN WINE

Chopped parsley
4 tablesps. oil, preferably
    olive oil
2 to 2 ½ cups vegetable
    stock

1 ½ pounds Jerusalem
    artichokes
Salt
Pinch of cayenne pepper
4 tablesps. sherry or ver-
    mouth

1. Pan parsley in hot fat for 3 minutes.
2. Add vegetable stock and bring to a boil.
3. Scrape artichokes, and place each artichoke into stock as soon as scraped.
4. Cover, and simmer for 20 minutes; season with salt and pepper and add wine.
5. Simmer for another 5 minutes or until vegetable is tender.

ASPARAGUS SOUFFLÉ

1 bunch cooked fresh
    asparagus or No. 2 or 2½
    can
2 eggs
¾ cup light sour cream

2 tablesps. chopped parsley
5 tablesps. grated cheese
Salt and white pepper, to
    taste
½ tablesp. oil

1. Cut cooked fresh or drained canned asparagus into 3-inch lengths.
2. Separate eggs.
3. Mix asparagus with sour cream, parsley, egg yolks and cheese; season to taste.
4. Beat egg whites stiff but not dry, and cut and fold into the mixture.
5. Place in a well-greased baking dish, and bake, uncovered, in a moderate oven for about 20 minutes.
6. Sprinkle with oil, and serve.

ASPARAGUS STEW

1 bunch fresh cooked asparagus or No. 2 or 2 ½ can	water
	Salt, red pepper, mace and nutmeg, to taste
1 medium onion	2 tablesps. brown sugar
2 tablesps. oil	1 medium potato
1 cup vegetable stock, or	2 teasps. lemon juice

1. Cut cooked fresh or drained canned asparagus into 3-inch lengths.

2. Chop onion, and pan in hot fat for 3 minutes.

3. Add asparagus, vegetable stock, seasoning and sugar; cover, and simmer over a low flame for 10 minutes.

4. Grate peeled raw potato, sprinkle with lemon juice, stir into vegetable, cover, and simmer for another 5 minutes.

CREAMED ASPARAGUS AU GRATIN

1 bunch fresh cooked asparagus, or No. 2 or 2 ½ can	1 tablesp. bread or cracker crumbs
1 cup medium white sauce	3 tablesp. cottage cheese or grated cheese
Salt, nutmeg and red pepper, to taste	1 tablesp. oil

1. Cut cooked fresh or drained canned asparagus into 3-inch lengths.

2. Place in a greased baking dish, and cover with white sauce seasoned with nutmeg, salt and a dash of red pepper.

3. Sprinkle with bread crumbs, cheese and oil, cover, and bake in a moderate oven for about 20 minutes.

FRENCH-FRIED ASPARAGUS

20 asparagus tips, 3 to 4 inches long	Salt and red pepper, to taste
Flour with	French pancake batter
	Oil for deep frying

1. Partially cook asparagus (3 to 5 minutes); the tips must be firm enough so that they can be handled without difficulty.

2. Drain and cool.

3. Dredge in well-seasoned flour.

4. Tie 3 to 4 into individual bundles and dip into batter until well covered.

5. Deep-fry in hot oil until crisp and golden brown.

6. Drain on paper and serve.

LIMA BEAN CASSEROLE

3 medium fresh tomatoes or 1 cup stewed	1 clove garlic
2 ½ cups shelled fresh lima beans	1 teasp. salt
	1 tablesp. oil
	Vegetable stock, or water

1. Cut up tomatoes, and mix with beans, garlic, salt and oil.

2. Barely cover with liquid, and simmer, covered, until beans are tender.

3. Remove garlic, and serve.

SAVORY LIMA BEANS

2 ½ cups shelled fresh lima beans	Salt and marjoram, to taste
Cheese sauce	Sprigs of mint or parsley

1. Cook beans until tender; drain, if necessary.

2. Mix with cheese sauce and season.

3. Garnish with mint or parsley and serve.

LIMA BEANS IN PEPPER SHELLS

2 cups shelled fresh lima
    beans
2 large green peppers
1 large onion
4 tablesps. oil or butter

2 to 3 tablesps. chopped
    pimiento, fresh or canned
Salt and paprika, to taste
Chopped parsley

1. Cook lima beans until tender; drain, if necessary.
2. Cut peppers in half lengthwise, remove seeds; cover with boiling water and parboil for 5 minutes. Drain.
3. Chop onion fine, and pan in 2 tablesps. hot fat until tender; add lima beans, pimiento and seasoning; blend well.
4. Fill pepper shells with mixture, sprinkle with parsley, dot with remaining fat, and bake, uncovered, in a moderate oven for 10 minutes.

LIMA BEANS O'BRIEN

2 ½ cups shelled fresh lima
    beans
3 canned pimientos
1 medium onion or 5 to 6
    scallions

2 tablesps. oil or pi-
    miento liquid
1 tablesp. chopped parsley
Salt and white pepper, to
    taste

1. Cook beans until tender; drain, if necessary.
2. Chop pimientos and onion, and pan in hot oil or pimiento liquid over a low flame for 5 minutes.
3. Add beans and parsley, season, mix well and heat thoroughly.

SOUR CREAM SUCCOTASH

1 to 1 ½ cups cooked fresh
   lima beans, or
2 cups quick-frozen baby
   limas, cooked
2 cups kernel corn, cooked

fresh or frozen
1 tablesp. oil or butter
1 cup sour cream
Salt and black pepper or
   sage, to taste

1. Heat corn and lima beans with butter in top of double boiler.

2. When thoroughly hot, stir in sour cream and seasoning. Heat thoroughly and serve.

SNAP OR WAX BEANS—ITALIAN STYLE

1 ½ pounds snap beans or
   2 pkgs. frozen
1 clove garlic
4 tablesps. oil
1 teasp. brown sugar
2 cups vegetable stock

Chopped parsley and chives
Salt and white pepper, to
   taste
1 tomato
1 hard-cooked egg

1. Cut fresh beans into thin strips lengthwise.

2. Cut garlic and rub with a little salt over the bottom of a saucepan. Add oil, parsley and sugar, and cook over a low flame for about 5 minutes, stirring frequently.

3. Add beans and cook for 5 minutes, add vegetable stock, cover, and simmer until almost tender.

4. Cook uncovered until all the liquid has evaporated and the beans are brown.

5. Season with white pepper, and garnish with sliced tomato and sliced hard-cooked egg. Sprinkle with chopped chives and serve.

This is also good if chilled and served cold; if served cold, garnish just before serving.

HUNGARIAN SNAP OR WAX BEANS

1 medium onion
3 tablesps. oil or butter
2 cups cooked fresh or frozen
    beans, cut diagonally
¼ cup vegetable stock, or
    water
1 teasp. sugar

2 fresh tomatoes or ½ cup
    canned, peeled and
    cubed
½ cup kernel corn, cooked
    fresh or frozen
1 small bay leaf
Salt and paprika, to taste
1 teasp. lemon juice

1. Chop onion, and pan in hot fat until tender.

2. Add beans and let brown; add vegetable stock and sugar, cover and simmer for 10 minutes.

3. Add tomatoes and corn, and simmer another 5 minutes.

4. Add bay leaf and cook an additional 5 minutes; remove bay leaf.

5. Season with salt, paprika and lemon juice, and serve.

SNAP OR WAX BEAN RAGOUT

1 ½ pounds beans
3 medium tomatoes
½ clove garlic
4 tablesps. oil
⅓ cup brown rice

1 tablesp. chopped dill or
    parsley
1 ½ cups vegetable stock
Salt and red pepper, to taste

1. String beans and cut crosswise into ½-inch pieces; cut up tomatoes.

2. Rub pot with garlic and salt. Heat oil in pot, add rice, and cook for 3 minutes, stirring constantly.

3. Add beans, dill or parsley, and tomatoes, and cook for 3 minutes.

4. Add vegetable stock, cover, and simmer for about 30 minutes, or until rice is tender.

5. Season to taste, and serve.

SNAP OR WAX BEANS WITH GREEN PEPPER

1 ½ pounds beans or 2 pkgs. cut frozen	Salt, paprika and savory, to taste
2 medium green peppers	3 tablesps. grated cheese or chopped peanuts
2 tablesps. oil	
2 cups vegetable stock	

1. Cut fresh beans in thin strips lengthwise.

2. Dip peppers into boiling water, remove seeds, and cut into thin strips lengthwise.

3. Heat oil in a saucepan, add beans and peppers and pan for 5 minutes.

4. Cover with vegetable stock, cover, and simmer until vegetables are tender.

5. Add salt, paprika and savory to taste. Sprinkle with cheese or chopped peanuts.

SOYBEAN SPROUTS IN SAUCE MOUSSELINE

2 cups soybean sprouts	butter
1 to 2 tablesps. oil or	1 cup sauce mousseline

1. Pan sprouts in hot oil over a very low flame for 1 minute; add 1 to 2 tablesps. hot water, cover, and cook for 10 minutes. Stir frequently. Drain if necessary.

2. Mix sprouts with sauce, blend well, and serve.

GREEN SOYBEAN CASSEROLE

½ cup cottage cheese	2 cups cooked fresh green
4 tablesps. milk	soybeans
Chopped parsley	Salt, paprika, nutmeg and
1 medium fresh tomato	marjoram, to taste
1 hard-cooked egg	2 to 3 tablesps. oil or
3 slices stale dark bread	butter

1. Cream cottage cheese with milk and parsley; break up or slice tomato; slice egg; grate bread.

2. Mix cheese with soybeans and season.

3. Place in well-greased baking dish, cover with tomato and bread and then sliced egg, sprinkle with oil, and bake, covered, in a moderate oven for about 20 minutes.

See also recipes for fresh Lima beans.

BEET CUSTARD

6 medium beets	2 eggs
Salt, to taste	½ cup milk
1 teasp. lemon juice	4 tablesps. grated cheese or
2 hard-cooked eggs	chopped peanuts
3 tablesps. oil	Chopped chives or parsley

1. Peel beets; if beets are young, they need not be peeled.

2. Shred on a fine shredder, and season with salt and lemon juice.

3. Slice hard-cooked eggs, and pan in hot fat for 2 minutes; line bottom of a baking dish with the eggs.

4. Stir beaten eggs into milk, add beets and cheese or peanuts, and mix well.

5. Pour mixture into baking dish, set in a pan of hot water, and bake, uncovered, in a moderate oven until set. To test, insert knive in custard; if it comes out clean, custard is set.

6. Sprinkle with chives or parsley and serve immediately.

BEETS AU GRATIN

3 cups sliced or diced cooked beets	Salt, if desired 4 to 6 tablesps. grated cheese
½ cup sour cream or plain yogurt	

1. Mix beets with cream in a well-greased shallow baking dish, season, and cover with cheese.

2. Place under moderate broiler until cheese is melted and beets thoroughly hot (about 10 to 15 minutes).

SPICY BEETS WITH APPLES

2 small onions	water
1 tablesp. oil	½ teasp. lemon juice
2 medium apples	Salt, nutmeg, basil, black
½ teasp. chopped caraway seeds	pepper, to taste
3 cups sliced cooked beets	2 tablesps. sour cream, if
½ cup vegetable stock, or	desired

1. Chop onion fine, and pan in hot fat until tender but not brown.

2. Core but do not peel apples, shred, preferably

on a glass or non-metallic shredder, add to onion together with caraway seeds; pan for 2 minutes.

3. Add sliced beets and enough liquid to prevent scorching, cover and simmer over a low flame for 10 minutes.

4. Season with lemon juice and spices to taste.

5. Mix well with sour cream, let come to a quick boil, and serve.

BEETS IN MADEIRA SAUCE

3 cups slices cooked beets   Sprigs of parsley
1 cup Madeira sauce

1. Drain beets if necessary; mix with Madeira sauce in top of double boiler, and heat thoroughly over boiling water.

2. Serve garnished with sprigs of parsley.

BEET GREENS

See recipes for Greens and Spinach.

BROCCOLI—ITALIAN STYLE

1 large bunch broccoli   Grated cheese, preferably
3 to 4 tablesps. oil   Parmesan type
2 tablesps. sherry or ver-
   mouth

1. Cook broccoli, and drain if necessary.

2. Heat oil, add wine, and simmer for 2 minutes, stirring occasionally.

3. Turn broccoli out on serving dish, pour sauce over it, and sprinkle with cheese.

BROCCOLI RING WITH STEWED TOMATOES

1 large bunch broccoli
½ cup thick white sauce or
    cream
2 eggs

2 tablesps. grated cheese.
Salt and red pepper, to taste
3 medium fresh tomatoes or
    1 cup stewed

1. Cook broccoli; drain if necessary, and chop coarsely.

2. Cool white sauce, or blend cream with beaten eggs; add broccoli, cheese, and seasoning.

3. Pour into well-greased ring mold, set in a pan of hot water, and bake, uncovered, in a moderate oven for about 35 minutes, or until set.

4. Stew or heat tomatoes while broccoli is baking.

5. Unmold broccoli, fill center with tomatoes, and serve.

BRUSSELS SPROUTS IN SOUR CREAM

1 ½ pounds Brussels
    sprouts
1 medium onion
3 tablesps. oil or butter
1 cup vegetable stock, or
    water

Salt, white pepper and mar-
    joram, to taste
½ cup sour cream or
    plain yogurt
Chopped chives or parsley

1. Blanch sprouts or let stand in cold salted water for 10 minutes; drain.

2. Chop onion and pan in hot fat until tender.

3. Add sprouts and cook over a low flame for 10 minutes, stirring frequently.

4. Add vegetable stock, cover, and simmer until tender.

5. Season to taste, add sour cream or yogurt; blend and reheat.

6. Garnish with chives or parsley, and serve.

FRENCH-FRIED BRUSSELS SPROUTS

1 pound Brussels sprouts
Salt and nutmeg, to taste
French pancake batter

Oil for deep frying
Tartar sauce or Spanish
   mayonnaise

1. Cook sprouts; drain if necessary and season.

2. Dip into batter until well covered, deep-fry in hot oil until crisp and golden brown, and drain on paper.

3. Serve with sauce in a separate dish.

SCALLOPED BRUSSELS SPROUTS

1 ½ pounds Brussels sprouts
2 leeks
2 tablesps. oil or butter
2 eggs
2 tablesps. milk

½ teasp. chopped parsley
Salt, paprika, chervil and
   basil, to taste
4 tablesps. bread or cracker
   crumbs

1. Cook sprouts; drain if necessary; chop leeks.

2. Heat 1 tablesp. fat, add sprouts and leeks, and pan over a low flame for about 5 minutes.

3. Mix thoroughly eggs, milk, parsley, and seasoning; pour over sprouts and blend well.

4. Turn mixture into well-greased baking dish; cover with bread or cracker crumbs, and dot with remaining fat.

5. Bake, uncovered, in a moderate oven for about 30 minutes, and serve.

CABBAGE GOULASH

1 medium head green cabbage
2 green peppers
4 to 5 tomatoes or 1 ½ cups stewed
2 tablesp. oil or butter
½ cup kernel corn, cooked fresh or frozen

Salt to taste
1 bay leaf
1 teasp. chopped caraway seeds
½ teasp. paprika
1 to 2 tablesps. sweet or sour cream, if desired

1. Cut cabbage into coarse pieces; dip green peppers into boiling water, remove seeds and cut into thin strips lengthwise. Chop or dice tomatoes.

2. Heat fat in a saucepan, add cabbage, tomatoes, peppers, corn and salt. Cover and simmer over a low flame for 15 minutes.

3. Add bay leaf, simmer for another 10 minutes, and remove bay leaf.

4. Season with caraway seeds and paprika, and add cream. Let come to a quick boil and serve.

CABBAGE IN SOUR CREAM

1 medium head cabbage, green or white
3 tablesps. oil
½ tablesp. caraway seeds
Salt, to taste
½ cup vegetable stock, or water

½ cup sour cream or plain yogurt
1 tablesp. oatmeal or grated cheese
1 medium onion, cut into rings

1. Shred or chop cabbage into coarse pieces.

2. Heat oil, add cabbage, sprinkle with caraway seeds and salt.

3. Add vegetable stock, cover, and simmer over a low flame for 20 minutes. If too dry, add additional vegetable stock or water to prevent scorching.

4. Turn into baking dish, stir in sour cream and oatmeal or cheese, cover with onion rings, and bake, uncovered, in a slow oven for 15 minutes.

STUFFED CABBAGE ROLLS

8 to 10 larger outer leaves of cabbage, green or white	1 egg yolk
½ pound mushrooms	1 tablesp. sour cream
1 small onion	Salt, red pepper, marjoram
5 to 6 tablesps. oil	or sage, to taste
1 cup oatmeal	½ cup tomato juice
	3 tablesps. grated cheese

1. Cover cabbage with boiling salted water and let stand for 5 minutes. Rinse and drain.

2. Slice mushrooms and chop onion.

3. Heat 3 tablesps. oil and pan mushrooms, onion, and oatmeal for 10 minutes. Stir constantly to prevent burning. Add 1 tablesp. of water, if necessary.

4. Cook slightly and stir in egg yolk slowly to prevent curdling, add sour cream, salt and seasoning.

5. Using 2 cabbage leaves for each roll, place 1 to 1 ½ tablesps. of stuffing in the center of each, roll and fasten with a toothpick, or tie with cord.

6. Place in a well-greased baking dish, pour tomato juice over rolls, sprinkle with remaining oil and bake, uncovered, in a moderate oven for 30 minutes.

7. Sprinkle with cheese, and serve.

CABBAGE IN WINE—ITALIAN STYLE

1 medium head cabbage, green or white	seeds
	Salt, to taste
2 to 3 tomatoes	½ cup white wine
1 medium onion	¼ teasp. lemon juice
2 tablesps. oil	Grated cheese, preferably
1 tablesp. chopped caraway	Parmesan type

1. Shred cabbage fine; peel and cube tomatoes; chop onion.

2. Heat fat, add onion and cabbage, and pan for 10 minutes.

3. Add caraway seeds and tomatoes, salt to taste, cover, and continue cooking for another 15 minutes.

4. Add wine and lemon juice, cover, and simmer an additional 10 minutes.

5. Serve with cheese in a separate dish.

CABBAGE STEW

1 medium head cabbage, green or white	seeds
	½ cup vegetable stock, or water
4 medium carrots	
2 single stalks of celery	1 bay leaf
2 to 3 tomatoes	Salt and black pepper, to taste
2 tablesps. oil	
1 tablesp. chopped caraway	

1. Shred cabbage, dice carrots, celery and tomatoes.

2. Melt fat, add vegetables and caraway seeds, and pan for 2 minutes.

3. Add vegetable stock, cover, and cook over a low flame until all vegetables are tender. Add bay leaf for last 10 minutes of cooking.

4. Remove bay leaf, place vegetables in serving dish, season with salt and pepper and serve.

CREAMED CHINESE CABBAGE WITH PARSLEY AND MINT

2 pounds Chinese cabbage
½ cup light cream
2 tablesps. chopped parsley
2 tablesps. chopped mint

leaves
1 teasp. oil
Salt and red pepper, to taste

1. Cut cabbage into small pieces, and cook for 8 minutes, or until tender. Drain if necessary.
2. Add remaining ingredients, cook for another 5 minutes, and serve.

PANNED RED CABBAGE

1 medium head red cabbage
1 medium onion
3 tablesps. oil or butter
1 cup vegetable stock, or water
Salt, caraway seeds, red

pepper, basil and nutmeg, to taste
2 tablesps brown sugar
1 potato
2 teasps. lemon juice

1. Shred or chop cabbage.
2. Chop onion fine, and pan in hot fat until tender.
3. Add cabbage and pan for 10 minutes, stirring occasionally.
4. Add stock, seasonings and sugar; cover and simmer over a low flame for 15 minutes.
5. Grate peeled potato, sprinkle immediately with lemon juice, and stir into cabbage, cover, and simmer until cabbage is tender.

RED CABBAGE FRITTERS

1 medium head red cabbage
French pancake batter
Salt, red pepper and mar-
joram, to taste
Oil for deep frying

1. Cut cabbage into eighths, leaving enough stem on each section to keep leaves from falling apart. Steam until tender; for this dish the cabbage must be steamed, not boiled in water.

2. Dip each section in pancake batter which has been seasoned to taste, and deep-fry in hot oil until golden brown.

3. Drain and serve.

RED CABBAGE WITH APPLES

1 medium head red cabbage
3 tart apples
3 tablesps. oil
½ cup vegetable stock, or
water
2 tablesps. brown sugar
1 teasp. chopped caraway
seeds
Salt, red pepper, to taste
Lemon juice
1 tablesp. grated horseradish

1. Shred cabbage fine; core and cube or slice apples.

2. Heat fat, add cabbage, apples and vegetable stock. Cover and simmer for 10 minutes.

3. Add sugar and seasonings. Cover and simmer for another 10 minutes or until cabbage is tender.

4. Add lemon juice to taste, sprinkle with horserad-ish, and serve.

CARROT AND PEPPER CASSEROLE

2 green peppers
3 tablesps. oil
3 cups sliced or diced car-
rots, cooked fresh or
canned or frozen
2 to 3 tablesps. sherry
Salt and nutmeg, to taste

1. Chop peppers and pan in hot fat over a low flame for 5 minutes.

2. Add carrots and wine, blend well and heat.

3. Season and serve.

CARROTS AND ASPARAGUS AU GRATIN

10 medium stalks asparagus, cooked

2 cups sliced or diced carrots, cooked fresh or canned or frozen

2 tablesps. chopped parsley

Salt and pepper or nutmeg, to taste

4 tablesps. cream, sweet or sour

4 tablesps. grated cheese

1. Cut asparagus into 1-inch pieces and mix with carrots, parsley and seasoned cream.

2. Place in shallow baking dish, cover with cheese, and bake, uncovered, in a moderate oven for about 20 minutes.

GLAZED CARROTS WITH GREEN PEAS

2 bunches young small carrots

½ cup vegetable stock, or water

2 tablesps. oil

2 cups cooked peas

Salt, paprika and marjoram, to taste

1 to 2 tablesps. brown sugar

Sprigs of parsley

1. Scrape and slice carrots in ½-inch rounds.

2. Cook in vegetable stock for 10 minutes over a very low flame. Drain, if necessary.

3. Heat oil, add carrots and peas, and pan for 5 minutes.

4. Add seasoning and sugar, and cook for 2 minutes. Stir occasionally to prevent sugar from scorching.

5. Garnish with sprigs of parsley, and serve.

MINTED CARROTS

1 ½ pounds carrots	1 to 2 tablesps. water
2 small or 1 medium onion	2 tablesps. chopped mint
4 tablesps. oil	leaves
2 tablesps. brown sugar	Salt and white pepper, to taste

1. Scrape carrots and cut in rounds about ½-inch thick.

2. Chop onions, and pan in hot fat until tender.

3. Add carrots, sugar and enough water to prevent burning, cover, and cook over a low flame for about 20 minutes, or until carrots are tender.

4. Blend in mint and seasoning, cook for another 5 minutes, and serve.

CAULIFLOWER AND MUSHROOM SOUFFLE

1 medium head cauliflower	Salt, nutmeg, paprika and
½ pound mushrooms	white pepper, to taste
1 cup medium white sauce	2 eggs
Chopped parsley	3 tablesps. bread or cracker
4 tablesps. grated cheese	crumbs
	1 tablesp. oil or butter

1. Cook cauliflower until tender; drain.

2. Chop mushrooms.

3. Break cauliflower into flowerets and mix with white sauce, mushrooms, parsley, and cheese; season to taste.

4. Separate eggs; beat yolks until light and creamy and beat whites until stiff but not dry.

5. Add egg yolks to cauliflower, blend well, and cut and fold in the egg whites.

6. Turn into well-greased baking dish, sprinkle with bread or cracker crumbs, dot with fat, cover and take in a moderate oven for about 25 minutes.

Serve immediately.

CAULIFLOWER FRITTERS

1 large head cauliflower	taste
2 medium potatoes	1 egg
¼ cup milk	3 tablesps. dry bread crumbs
Salt and white pepper, to	Oil for frying

1. Cook cauliflower; drain if necessary, and break into flowerets.

2. Cook and mash potatoes.

3. Mix milk with seasoning; add cauliflower and blend well; add mashed potatoes and mix thoroughly. Shape into patties.

4. Dip in well-beaten egg, then roll in bread crumbs.

5. Deep-fry in hot oil on both sides until golden brown. Turn only once.

Serve immediately.

CAULIFLOWER—ITALIAN STYLE

1 large head cauliflower	Salt and marjoram, to taste
4 tablesps. oil	1 hard-cooked egg
4 tablesps. tomato paste	Grated dry cheese

1. Cook cauliflower; drain if necessary, and leave whole.

2. Blend oil with tomato paste and seasoning.

3. Place cauliflower in a well-greased baking dish, cover with tomato sauce, and bake, covered, in a moderate oven for 15 minutes. Uncover and bake for another 10 minutes.

4. Garnish with egg slices, sprinkle with cheese, and serve.

BRAISED CELERY—MEXICAN STYLE

1 large bunch green or white celery
3 medium potatoes
1 large onion
1 medium tomato
6 black olives

4 tablesps. oil
Salt, marjoram and red pepper or pimiento, to taste
3 to 4 tablesps. water, if necessary

1. Cut celery into 1-inch pieces; cook potatoes; slice onion; slice or chop tomato; chop olives.
2. Heat oil, add celery and onion, and pan over a low flame for about 5 minutes. Stir frequently.
3. Add tomato, olives and seasoning.
4. Cover, and simmer over a very low flame until vegetable is tender; if necessary, add 3 to 4 tablesps. water.
5. Slice potatoes, place on a warm platter, cover with celery, and serve.

CELERY O'BRIEN

1 large bunch green or white celery
1 large onion
½ green pepper
3 tablesps. oil

4 tablesps. chopped pimiento, fresh or canned
Salt and red pepper, to taste
Tomato juice, if necessary

1. Cut celery into 1-inch pieces, cook, drain, if necessary.
2. Chop onion and green pepper, and pan in hot oil for 5 minutes.
3. Add celery and pimiento, blend well and season. Cover and cook over low heat until vegetable is brown. Stir several times to brown on all sides (about 15 to 20 minutes). Moisten with a little tomato juice if too dry.

CELERY—RUSSIAN STYLE

1 large bunch green or white celery	seeds
	Salt, to taste
2 tablesps. oil	1 teasp. flour
1 cup cooked beets, sliced or diced	½ cup sour cream
	1 tablesp. grated horseradish
½ tablesp. chopped caraway	

1. Slice celery in 1-inch pieces, and pan in hot oil for 10 minutes, using a very low flame.

2. Add beets, caraway seeds and salt, and continue panning for another 5 minutes.

3. Blend flour and cream, stir into celery, and allow to come to a quick boil.

4. Serve, sprinkled with horseradish.

CELERY KNOB AU GRATIN

2 medium celery knobs (about 1 ½ pounds)	4 tablesps. oil
	Salt and paprika, to taste
1 pound spinach or romaine	3 to 4 tablesps. grated cheese

1. Cook celery knob until tender; slice.

2. Cut spinach or romaine into fine strips, and pan in 3 tablesps. hot oil for 5 minutes; season.

3. Place half of celery in well-greased baking dish, cover with spinach or romaine and top with remaining celery.

4. Sprinkle with cheese and with remaining oil.

5. Bake, uncovered, in a moderate oven for 10 minutes; or place under moderate broiler until it is thoroughly heated and cheese is melted.

CELERY KNOB DUMPLINGS

2 medium celery knobs
    (about 1 ½ pounds)
Lemon juice
5 to 6 slices day-old bread
Chopped parsley, to taste
2 tablesps. oil

1 egg
½ cup milk
Salt, to taste
2 to 3 tablesps. flour
2 tablesps. bread or cracker
    crumbs

1. Peel celery knob, shred, and sprinkle with lemon juice; cube bread.
2. Heat 1 tablesp. oil, add bread and parsley, and fry until bread cubes are crisp and slightly brown.
3. Add to celery and mix well.
4. Blend beaten egg with milk; pour over celery mixture and allow to stand for 5 minutes.
5. Add salt, and enough flour to make mixture firm.
6. Shape into small balls with wet hands. Drop into rapidly boiling, salted water, cover, and cook for 10 minutes without lifting the lid.
7. Brown bread or cracker crumbs in 1 tablesp. oil.
8. Remove dumplings, drain, roll in crumbs, and serve.

CELERY KNOB PILAF

2 medium celery knobs
    (about 1 ½ pounds)
¾ cups brown rice

1 ½ cups stewed tomatoes
3 tablesps. oil
Salt and paprika, to taste

1. Cook and dice celery. Cook rice, and drain, if necessary.
2. Mix rice with celery, tomatoes and oil, and heat, uncovered, over very low flame until thoroughly heated.
3. Season to taste, and serve.

CELERY KNOB—ITALIAN STYLE

1 cup vegetable stock, or
    water
4 tablesps. tomato paste
2 medium celery knobs
    (about 1 ½ pounds)
1 fresh pimiento or 2 small
    canned

1 tablesp. oil
Salt and nutmeg or paprika,
    to taste
Chopped parsley
4 to 6 tablesps. grated
    cheese, Parmesan type

1. Mix liquid with tomato paste and heat to boiling.
2. Peel thin and slice celery directly into boiling liquid, cover, and simmer for 10 minutes.
3. Chop pimiento, pan in hot oil for 5 minutes, and add to celery.
4. Season and simmer for another 10 minutes or until celery is tender.
5. Turn out on serving dish, sprinkle with parsley and cheese, and serve.

SWISS CHARD CASSEROLE

1 large bunch Swiss chard
    (about 2 pounds)
1 green pepper
2 cups kernel corn, cooked
    fresh or frozen
3 tablesps. chopped pimiento

½ cup milk
1 cup vegetable stock, or
    water
Salt and white pepper, to
    taste
1 tablesp. oil

1. Cut leaves and stalks of Swiss chard into small pieces; chop green pepper.
2. Place chard in well-greased baking dish. Cover with a layer of corn; make a mixture of pepper and pimiento a third layer.
3. Mix milk with vegetable stock and seasoning. Pour over vegetable.

4. Sprinkle with oil, cover, and bake in a moderate oven for about 40 minutes.

Serve immediately.

SCALLOPED SWISS CHARD

1 large bunch Swiss chard (about 2 pounds)
1 single stalk of celery
½ cup sour cream or medium white sauce
Salt, chervil and nutmeg, to taste
½ cup vegetable stock, or water
Chopped chives

1. Cut stems from the leaves of Swiss chard; slice leaves and chop stems; chop celery.

2. Mix with either sour cream or white sauce and seasoning.

3. Place in a well-greased baking dish, blend with vegetable stock and bake, covered, in a moderate oven for about 35 minutes.

4. Sprinkle with chives, and serve.

See also recipes for Spinach.

FRIED CHAYOTES

1 ½ pounds chayotes
Flour
Salt and nutmeg, to taste
1 egg
Bread or cracker crumbs
Oil for deep frying

1. Cook chayotes and drain.

2. Cut in half lengthwise without peeling or removing seed.

3. Dip in seasoned flour, then in beaten egg, and then in crumbs until well coated.

4. Deep-fry in hot oil until golden brown, drain on paper, and serve, preferably with a sauce such as curry, mustard or cheese sauce.

See also recipes for Cucumber and Summer Squash.

SPICED CHESTNUTS

1 ½ pounds chestnuts
1 medium onion
2 to 3 tablesps. oil
2 medium ripe tomatoes

Salt, savory and nutmeg, to taste
Chopped chives

1. Cook chestnuts
2. Chop onion and cut up tomatoes.
3. Pan onion in hot oil until tender; add tomatoes and seasoning, cover, and simmer for 5 minutes.
4. Add chestnuts, and simmer for another 5 minutes.
5. Place on platter, sprinkle with chives, and serve.

COLLARDS—ITALIAN STYLE

2 pounds collards
1 clove garlic
2 to 3 tablesps. oil
1 cup tomato juice
1 cup vegetable stock, or

water
1 medium onion
Salt, marjoram and black pepper, to taste
2 tablesps. grated cheese

1. Cut collards into large, coarse shreds.
2. Rub pan with cut clove of garlic and heat oil. Add tomato juice and vegetable stock, and let come to a boil.

3. Add collards and whole onion, cover, and simmer for 10 minutes.

4. Remove onion and season. Cover and simmer for another 5 minutes or until tender.

5. Serve, sprinkled with cheese.

CORN AU GRATIN

1 large onion	Salt and marjoram, to taste
2 tablesps. oil	3 to 4 tablesps. milk
3 cups kernel corn, cooked fresh or frozen	3 tablesps. grated cheese

1. Slice onion into rings, and pan in hot oil for about 5 minutes.

2. Place half of onions in shallow baking dish, add corn, seasoning, and enough milk to moisten the corn thoroughly. Cover with onion rings, and sprinkle with cheese.

3. Place under moderate broiler until cheese is melted and corn thoroughly hot (about 10 to 15 minutes).

BAKED CORN—HUNGARIAN STYLE

8 black pitted olives	2 teasps. chopped parsley
3 cups kernel corn, cooked fresh or frozen	Salt, paprika, cayenne pepper and nutmeg, to taste
1 cup medium white sauce	
2 tablesps. tomato paste	Chopped peanuts, if desired

1. Chop olives.

2. Mix corn with white sauce, tomato paste, parsley,

olives, and seasoning.

3. Place in well-greased baking dish, cover, and bake in a moderate oven for about 20 minutes.

4. Sprinkle with peanuts, and serve.

CORN FRITTERS

2 eggs	2 cups kernel corn, cooked
½ cup flour	fresh or frozen
½ teasp. salt	Oil for deep fat frying
½ teasp. baking powder	2 tablesps. grated dry cheese
¼ teasp. white pepper	
Chopped parsley	

1. Separate eggs; beat egg yolks until light; beat egg whites until stiff but not dry.

2. Sift together all dry ingredients, except grated cheese.

3. Add well-drained corn and egg yolks to dry ingredients, and blend well.

4. Cut and fold in egg whites.

5. Shape into small fritters.

6. Deep-fry in hot oil until golden brown, drain; sprinkle with grated cheese, and serve.

DEVILED CORN

4 medium tomatoes	3 cups kernel corn, cooked
4 tablesps. oil	fresh or frozen
Salt and black pepper, to	3 tablesps. grated cheese
taste	1 teasp. prepared mustard

1. Cut tomatoes in half, dot with a little butter, season, and put under medium broiler for 10 minutes.

2. Mix corn with cheese, mustard, and remaining oil, and heat thoroughly.

3. Turn out on a platter, surround with broiled tomatoes, and serve immediately.

HUNGARIAN CUCUMBER STEW

3 medium cucumbers (about 1 ½ pounds)
3 large fresh tomatoes or 1 ½ cups stewed
1 medium onion
2 tablesps. oil
Salt, black pepper and marjoram, to taste
Bay leaf
½ cup sour cream or plain yogurt
1 tablesp. flour
Chopped dill

1. Peel cucumbers, cut in half, remove seeds, and cut into small pieces, or dice. Chop or slice tomatoes; chop onion fine.

2. Pan onion in hot oil until tender; add cucumbers and tomatoes, season, add bay leaf, cover, and simmer for 15 minutes.

3. Remove bay leaf; blend sour cream with flour and dill, stir into vegetable, let come to a quick boil, and serve.

STUFFED CUCUMBERS

2 large cucumbers
½ pound mushrooms
5 tablesps. oil
Chopped parsley, to taste
½ cup cooked rice, or
6 tablesps. oatmeal and 2 tablesps. chopped nuts
Salt, to taste
2 firm tomatoes
3 tablesps. grated cheese

1. Pare cucumbers, cut lengthwise into halves and hollow out centers.

2. Remove seeds, and chop remaining pulp.

3. Cut mushrooms and pan in 3 tablesps. hot oil for 5 minutes; add cucumber pulp, parsley and rice (or oatmeal and nuts), and pan for another 5 minutes; season with salt.

4. Stuff cucumber shells.

5. Slice tomatoes, place over stuffed cucumbers, and dot with remaining oil.

6. Place in well-greased baking dish; bake, uncovered, in a moderate oven for 15 minutes or until well-browned.

7. Sprinkle with cheese, and serve.

SCALLOPED DASHEENS

1 pound dasheens
1 large ripe tomato
½ cup medium white sauce
   or sour cream
½ teasp. brown sugar

Pinch of cinnamon
Salt, nutmeg and white pepper, to taste
4 tablesps. chopped peanuts

1. Cook, peel and slice dasheens; place in well-greased baking dish.

2. Cut up tomato and mix thoroughly with white sauce, sugar and other seasonings.

3. Cover dasheens with mixture and sprinkle with peanuts.

4. Bake, uncovered, in a moderate oven for about 20 minutes.

See also recipes for Potatoes except mashed.

EGGPLANT AU GRATIN

1 large eggplant
Lemon juice
Salt and white pepper, to

taste
4 tablesps. light cream
½ cup grated cheese

1. Parboil unpeeled eggplant for 5 minutes, dry and cut into ½-inch thick slices lengthwise, rub immediately with lemon juice.

2. Place in a shallow baking dish and season.

3. Mix cream with cheese and pour over eggplant.

4. Place under moderate broiler for about 20 minutes or until cheese is melted and top brown. Serve soon.

EGGPLANT—DALMATIAN STYLE

1 large eggplant	3 tablesps. oil
Lemon juice	½ cup kernel corn, cooked fresh or frozen
1 large onion	
2 green peppers	Salt, paprika or allspice, and cayenne pepper, to taste
3 ripe tomatoes or 1 cup stewed	
1 clove garlic	4 tablesps. light cream, if desired

1. Wash and dice unpeeled eggplant. Sprinkle immediately with lemon juice.

2. Chop onion, peppers and tomatoes coarsely.

3. Rub bottom of saucepan with a cut clove of garlic and salt, pour in oil, and pan onion in it until tender. Add tomatoes and eggplant, cover, and simmer for about 10 minutes.

4. Add green peppers and corn, and season; cover and simmer for another 10 minutes, or until eggplant is tender.

5. Blend with light cream, if desired, let come to a quick boil, and serve.

EGGPLANT GOULASH

4 medium mushrooms	1 large eggplant
3 medium fresh tomatoes or 1 cup stewed	Lemon juice
	Salt, paprika and marjoram, to taste
2 green peppers	
3 tablesps. oil	4 tablesps. wine

1. Chop mushrooms, tomatoes and peppers coarsely.

2. Heat oil in saucepan.

3. Dice eggplant unpeeled and add to oil as cut; add a few drops of lemon juice. Stir well. Add mushroom, tomatoes and green peppers. Cover, and simmer over a low flame for about 20 minutes or until tender.

4. Season and add wine. Simmer for another 5 minutes and serve.

EGGPLANT—SPANISH STYLE

1 clove garlic
5 tablesps. oil
1 tablesp. chopped parsley
1 large eggplant

1 fresh pimiento or 1 small can, chopped
Lemon juice
Salt and red pepper, to taste

1. Rub bottom of pan with cut clove of garlic and salt; heat oil, and pan parsley for 3 minutes.

2. Cut eggplant unpeeled into 1-inch cubes, put into hot oil as cut, cover, and cook over a low flame for 10 minutes, after all the eggplant is in. Add pimiento. Stir carefully a few times.

3. Season with lemon juice and seasoning, and serve. Can be eaten either hot or cold.

STUFFED EGGPLANT

1 large or 2 small eggplants
Lemon juice
1 cup cooked peas
½ clove garlic, mashed
¼ pound mushrooms,

chopped
Salt, marjoram, chervil and tarragon, to taste
2 ripe tomatoes, sliced
1 tablesp. oil

1. Cut slice from top of eggplant; cut, unpeeled, into half lengthwise, hollow out centers with a spoon, leaving a ¾-inch-thick shell. Sprinkle immediately with lemon juice.

2. Chop pulp coarsely and mix with peas, garlic and mushrooms; season, and stuff eggplant shells with the mixture.

3. Place in well-greased baking dish, top with sliced tomatoes; sprinkle with oil. Pour a little liquid in the bottom of baking dish.

4. Bake, uncovered, in a moderate oven for 25 minutes.

FRENCH ENDIVE IN MADEIRA SAUCE

1 pound endive (French)   Salt and paprika, to taste
1 cup Madeira sauce

1. Cover endive with boiling, slightly salted water, and simmer, covered, until tender. Drain.

2. Mix endive with sauce, blend well, season. If necessary, reheat over boiling water.

ESCAROLE WITH MUSHROOMS

2 medium heads escarole   3 tablesps. oil
2 medium fresh tomatoes or   Salt, to taste
   ½ cup stewed   1 cup vegetable stock, or
1 green pepper   water
1 medium potato, cooked   3 to 4 tablesps. sherry
4 medium mushrooms   1 tablesp. chopped parsley

1. Cut escarole into coarse strips; quarter tomatoes; cut pepper into strips; slice or dice potato; slice or quarter mushrooms.

2. Pan all vegetables in hot oil for 5 minutes.

3. Season, add enough vegetable stock to barely cover, and simmer, covered, for 15 minutes or until escarole is tender.

4. Add wine, let come to a quick boil, sprinkle with parsley, and serve.

FENNEL RISOTTO

1 ½ pounds fennel
2 medium onions
½ pound mushrooms
3 tablesps. oil

Salt
1 cup uncooked brown rice
Grated cheese, preferably
    Parmesan type, to taste

1. Cook fennel in 6 cups water until tender; drain, and save cooking water. Keep fennel water hot over a low flame until used. Chop fennel coarsely.

2. Chop onions fine; cut mushrooms into small pieces.

3. Pan onions in hot fat until tender (in saucepan in which rice is to be cooked); add mushrooms, and cook over a low flame for about 5 minutes. Season with salt.

4. Add rice (cleaned but not washed) and brown slightly, stirring constantly.

5. Add 4 to 5 tablesps. fennel water and stir with a wooden spoon until water is absorbed. Repeat, stirring constantly, and keep on adding water each time rice becomes dry. Risotto is ready when it has been stirred for 18 minutes.

6. Remove from flame, add chopped fennel and mix well.

7. Turn out on serving dish, sprinkle with cheese, and serve.

"GREENS" OMELET

2 cups cooked greens (about 2 pounds), such as dandelions, lamb's quarters, mustard, sorrel, or chicory; or endive, escarole and field lettuce

1 egg
3 to 4 tablesps. light cream
Salt, pepper and mace, to taste
2 tablesps. oil

1. Mix greens, egg, cream and seasoning into smooth batter.

2. Cook in frying pan in hot oil like omelet.
   Serve immediately.

BAKED "GREENS"

1 large bunch beet or turnip greens (1 ½ to 2 pounds)
1 medium onion
3 medium ripe tomatoes or 1 cup stewed
3 tablesps. oatmeal or cracker crumbs

Salt, celery salt, nutmeg and savory, to taste
½ cup sour cream or plain yogurt
¼ cup vegetable stock, or water
2 tablesps. chopped peanuts

1. Shred leaves and chop stalks of greens; chop onion; chop or dice tomatoes.

2. Mix thoroughly the greens, onion, tomatoes, and oatmeal or cracker crumbs, and season to taste.

3. Place in well-greased baking dish, and blend well with sour cream and vegetable stock; if yogurt is used, less stock is needed.

4. Cover and bake in a moderate oven for about 30 minutes; uncover, and bake for another 10 minutes.

5. Sprinkle with peanuts, and serve.

BAKED KALE WITH POTATOES

1 ½ pounds kale
4 medium potatoes
2 to 3 cups vegetable stock, or water
1 tablesp. chopped parsley

1 bay leaf
Salt and black pepper, to taste
Grated cheese, if desired

1. Blanch kale and chop coarsely; peel potatoes and cut in halves or quarters.

2. Barely cover kale and potatoes with liquid, add parsley and bay leaf, cover, and simmer for 10 minutes.

3. Remove bay leaf, season, stir well, cover, and simmer until vegetables are tender (10 to 15 minutes).

4. Serve sprinkled with cheese.

KALE FRITTERS

1 pound kale	2 to 3 tablesps. sour cream
½ cup cooked brown rice	Flour
Salt, red pepper and savory, to taste	Oil for frying

1. Cook kale until tender; drain if necessary, and chop coarsely.

2. Mix with rice, and season; add enough sour cream to make a firm mixture, and shape into fritters.

3. Roll in flour, and fry in hot oil until golden brown, turning only once.

Serve with a well-seasoned sauce.

KALE WITH TOMATOES

2 pounds kale	1 cup vegetable stock, or water
4 large ripe tomatoes or 2 cups stewed	1 teasp. brown sugar
8 black olives	Salt and marjoram, to taste
1 tablesp. oil	

1. Blanch kale and chop coarsely; cut up tomatoes; pit and chop olives.

2. Pan tomatoes in hot oil for 3 minutes, add kale, olives, and enough liquid to prevent scorching; cover and simmer for 10 minutes.

3. Add sugar and seasoning, stir well, cover and simmer until kale is tender (10 to 15 minutes).

SCALLOPED KALE

2 pounds kale	Salt and nutmeg, to taste
2 eggs	1 clove garlic
1 cup medium white sauce or sour cream	3 tablesps. bread or cracker crumbs
1 cup cooked soybeans	1 tablesp. oil

1. Blanch kale and chop coarsely.

2. Separate eggs; beat yolks until light and whites until stiff but not dry.

3. Stir yolks and seasoning into white sauce.

4. Mix kale and soybeans with white sauce mixture, and cut and fold in egg whites.

5. Rub baking dish with cut clove of garlic, and grease well. Fill with kale, cover with bread crumbs, sprinkle with oil, and bake, uncovered, in a moderate oven for about 35 minutes.

Serve immediately.

KOHLRABI À LA CREOLE

4 large or 8 small kohlrabi	2 fresh tomatoes or ½ cup stewed
4 large mushrooms	
1 green pepper	Salt and black pepper, to taste
1 small onion	
6 to 8 black olives	Vegetable stock or water
3 tablesps. oil	Sherry, to taste

1. Cook, peel and dice kohlrabi.

2. Chop mushrooms, pepper and onion; pit and chop olives.

3. Pan mushrooms, pepper, onion and olives in hot oil for 10 minutes.

4. Add kohlrabi and tomatoes, season, and heat thoroughly. Moisten with vegetable stock if necessary.

5. Add sherry, stir well, and serve.

KOHLRABI IN SOUR CREAM

4 large or 8 small kohlrabi
1 cup sour cream or
    plain yogurt

2 tablesps. oil
Salt, nutmeg and black pepper, to taste

1. Cook, drain and dice kohlrabi.
2. Heat oil in a saucepan, add sour cream and seasoning.
3. Add kohlrabi; bring to a boil; cover and heat if necessary. Serve immediately.

FRIED KOHLRABI SLICES

4 large kohlrabi
Salt, celery salt and savory,
    to taste

Drop batter
Oil for deep frying
2 to 3 tablesps. grated
cheese

1. Cook and peel kohlrabi; cut into ½-inch slices. Cool slightly.
2. Season and dip into batter until well covered.
3. Deep-fry in hot oil until golden brown.
4. Drain, sprinkle with cheese, and serve.

LEEKS AU GRATIN

1 large bunch leeks
Salt, to taste
1 teasp. chopped caraway

seeds
4 tablesps. grated cheese
2 tablesps. oil

1. Cook leeks, and drain if necessary. Cut into desired shape to fit into shallow baking dish.
2. Grease baking dish, fill with leeks, sprinkle with salt, caraway seeds and cheese, and dot with oil.
3. Place under moderate broiler until cheese is melted and vegetable is thoroughly hot, about 10 to 15 minutes.

LEEKS—HUNGARIAN STYLE

1 large bunch leeks
3 large fresh tomatoes or
    1 ½ cups stewed
½ clove garlic

3 tablesps. oil
½ cup vegetable stock, or
    liquid from tomatoes
Salt and paprika, to taste
2 to 3 tablesp. bread crumbs

1. Slice leeks and cut up tomatoes.

2. Rub pan with garlic and salt, and heat 2 tablesps. oil.

3. Pan leeks and tomatoes in hot oil over a low flame for 10 minutes, add liquid and seasoning, cover, and simmer until tender (10 to 15 minutes).

4. Blend bread crumbs with 1 tablesp. oil, sprinkle over leeks, and serve.

BAKED LEEKS—RUSSIAN STYLE

3 to 4 slices stale rye or
    pumpernickel bread
½ cup sour cream
1 large bunch leeks
3 tablesps. oil

1 hard-cooked egg
¼ teasp. prepared mustard
Salt and nutmeg, to taste
3 tablesps. grated horse-
    radish or pickled beets

1. Grate bread and mix with sour cream.

2. Cut leeks into ½-inch lengths, and pan in hot oil for 10 minutes on a very low flame; season.

3. Chop egg, mix with mustard and seasoning; blend into sour cream.

4. Place leeks in well-greased baking dish, cover with sour cream mixture, and bake, covered, in a moderate oven for about 20 minutes.

5. Sprinkle with horseradish, and serve.

LETTUCE SQUABS

1 small head of lettuce or 8 to 10 large lettuce leaves Sprigs of parsley or chives	French pancake batter Oil for deep frying Salt, marjoram and red pepper, to taste

1. Thoroughly dry lettuce leaves.
2. Tie 2 or 3 leaves at one end with a sprig of parsley or a chive, and dip into batter until well covered.
3. Drop into hot oil and deep-fry until golden brown.
4. Drain on paper, season to taste, and serve.

See also recipe for Braised Romaine.

FRIED VEGETABLE MARROW

2 or 3 medium vegetable marrows (about 1 ½ pounds) ½ teasp. celery salt Salt and paprika, to taste	Flour Drop batter Oil for deep frying 4 tablesps. grated cheese

1. Peel marrow only if skin is tough, and cut into fairly thick slices, discarding centers, if seeds are large. Season, and dredge with flour.
2. Dip into batter until well covered, and deep-fry in hot oil until golden brown.
3. Drain on paper, sprinkle with cheese, and serve.

See also recipes for Summer Squash and Zucchini.

BULGARIAN MUSHROOMS

1 ½ pounds mushrooms
½ cup yogurt or sour cream
2 tablesps. oil
2 tablesps. milk

Chopped parsley
Salt and red pepper, to taste
3 tablesps. chopped nut-
   meats

1. Quarter mushrooms, leaving stems on.

2. Heat together yogurt, oil, milk and parsley; do not boil.

3. Add mushrooms and seasoning, cover, and simmer over a very low flame until mushrooms are tender (about 20 minutes); do not allow to boil.

4. Mix with nutmeats and serve.

MUSHROOMS AU GRATIN

1 ½ pounds mushrooms
4 hard-cooked eggs
1 small onion
4 tablesps. cream, sweet or
   sour, and
4 tablesps. grated American

cheese or
½ cup quick cheese sauce
4 tablesps. oil
Salt and red pepper, to taste
Chopped parsley
4 shells, if desired

1. Slice mushrooms; chop eggs and onions separately; mix cream with grated cheese.

2. Pan onion and mushrooms in 3 tablesps. hot oil on a very low flame for 8 minutes; stir occasionally.

3. Add cream and cheese mixture, or stir in cheese sauce; season, and blend well.

4. Fill into greased baking dish or individual ramekins, sprinkle with remaining oil, and broil under medium broiler for about 15 minutes, or until light brown.

5. Sprinkle with parsley, and serve.

MUSHROOMS À LA PROVENCALE

1 medium onion or 5 or 6 scallions	1 tablesp. flour
1 ½ pounds mushrooms	Salt and red pepper, to taste
3 tablesps. oil	1 clove garlic
	½ cup white wine

1. Chop onion or grate scallions fine; slice mushrooms; pan both in hot oil over a low flame for about 5 minutes, stirring constantly.

2. Stir in flour and spices, and add uncut clove garlic; add wine, cover, and simmer over a very low flame for about 10 minutes, or until mushrooms are tender.

3. Remove garlic and serve.

MUSHROOMS—CHINESE STYLE

1 pound mushrooms	2 tablesps. flour
½ clove garlic	Salt and white pepper, to taste
3 tablesps. oil	Chopped parsley
4 eggs	3 firm tomatoes
½ cup light cream	

1. Peel mushrooms if necessary, and chop.

2. Rub shallow pan with garlic and salt, heat oil, and pan mushrooms on a very low flame for 5 minutes.

3. Separate eggs; mix yolks with cream, flour and seasoning, and beat whites stiff but not dry.

4. Add yolk mixture to mushrooms, blend well, and cut and fold in egg whites. Cover and cook over a low flame for 3 minutes.

5. Turn with a spatula and cook for 2 minutes on the other side.

6. Turn out on a warm platter, sprinkle with parsley and garnish with sliced tomatoes.

MUSHROOM GOULASH

1 to 1 ½ pounds mushrooms
1 large onion
2 tablesps. oil
3 large fresh tomatoes or
   1 ½ cups stewed
½ cup kernel corn, cooked
   fresh or frozen

1 bay leaf
Salt, nutmeg and marjoram,
   to taste
½ cup sour cream, if de-
   sired
1 tablesp. chopped parsley

1. Quarter or slice mushrooms without peeling, and chop or slice onion.

2. Pan onion in hot fat until crisp and light brown; add mushrooms, cover, and simmer over a low flame for 5 minutes.

3. Cut up tomatoes, add and cook for 5 minutes; add corn, bay leaf, season, cover, and cook for an additional 5 minutes. If stewed tomatoes are used, add together with corn.

4. Remove bay leaf; add sour cream and parsley, bring to a quick boil, and serve.

MUSHROOMS IN CREAM

1 ½ pounds mushrooms
2 tablesps. oil or butter
Salt and red pepper, to taste
1 cup light cream

1 teasp. flour
Chopped parsley or dill or
   chives

1. Slice mushrooms and pan in hot fat for about 5 minutes; season.

2. Mix cream with flour and stir into mushrooms; let come to a quick boil.

3. Place under medium broiler for 10 minutes.

4. Serve sprinkled with parsley, dill or chives.

MUSHROOMS IN BATTER

1 ½ pounds very large
    mushrooms
French pancake batter
Oil for deep frying

Salt, to taste
Pinch of cayenne pepper
2 firm tomatoes
1 small lemon

1. Peel and cut mushrooms in halves, leaving stems on.

2. Dip in batter and deep-fry in hot oil until golden brown. Drain on paper. Season.

3. Serve garnished with slices of tomato and lemon.

MUSHROOMS—PEASANT STYLE

3 medium potatoes
2 cups vegetable stock or
    water
1 ½ pounds mushrooms
1 medium cucumber

Salt and marjoram, to taste
1 to 2 tablesps. flour, if necessary
1 teasp. vinegar, if desired

1. Peel and dice potatoes and cook in vegetable stock for 10 minutes.

2. Quarter or slice mushrooms; slice cucumber (unpeeled if young and not bitter); add both to potatoes; season.

3. Cover and simmer until potatoes are tender.

4. If liquid is too thin, stir in 1 or 2 tablesps. flour and let come to a quick boil, stirring constantly. Add vinegar if a sour taste is desired.

MUSHROOM RISOTTO

4 tablesps. oil
1 cup brown rice
3 ½ cups vegetable stock,
    or water
½ medium onion
1 pound mushrooms

½ cup stewed tomatoes
6 black olives
Salt and pepper, to taste
½ cup cooked peas
4 tablesps. grated cheese

1. Heat 2 tablesps: oil, add rice and pan for about 5 minutes, stirring constantly.

2. Put in top of double boiler with 3 cups hot stock and whole onion, cover, and cook for 15 minutes.

3. Slice mushrooms; cut up tomatoes; pit and chop olives.

4. Heat remaining fat and pan mushrooms, tomatoes and olives for 15 minutes; season.

5. Add to rice, stir well, and finish cooking until rice is tender. Blend in peas.

6. Sprinkle with cheese, and serve.

OKRA AU GRATIN

1 pound okra	½ cup tomato juice
2 green peppers	4 tablesps. grated cheese
Salt and pepper, to taste	

1. Slice okra and cut off stems; cook until tender; drain.

2. Chop pepper very fine and mix with okra; season.

3. Place in greased shallow baking dish, cover with tomato juice and sprinkle with cheese.

4. Place under moderate broiler until cheese is melted and vegetable is thoroughly hot (about 12 to 15 minutes).

SCALLION CUSTARD (GREEN ONIONS)

2 bunches scallions	1 teasp. flour
¾ cup milk	Salt, sage or savory, to taste
1 egg	1 teasp. brown sugar

1. Trim off any wilted parts, and parboil scallions for 5 minutes; drain and chop.

2. Mix milk with beaten egg in top of double boiler, and cook over boiling water. Stir in flour, blend well and season.

3. When mixture begins to thicken, add scallions and sugar, cover, and cook until custard is set.

ONIONS BAKED IN WINE

2 to 3 large Bermuda-type onions
½ cup light cream
1 teasp. brown sugar
Vermouth or sherry, to taste
Salt and cinnamon, to taste

1. Cut onions in thick slices and arrange in greased baking dish.

2. Mix cream with sugar and wine to taste, pour over onions, and sprinkle with salt and cinnamon.

3. Bake, uncovered, in a slow oven for about 35 minutes. Baste several times.

Serve with liquid.

FRENCH-FRIED ONIONS—SWEDISH STYLE

1 pound silverskin onions
Drop batter
Oil for deep frying
Salt
3 tablesps. grated cheese

1. Parboil onions for 5 minutes, drain, and dry thoroughly.

2. Dip into drop batter.

3. Deep-fry in hot oil until golden brown. Drain on paper.

4. Sprinkle with salt and cheese, and serve.

SPANISH ONIONS WITH NUTS

4 large Spanish-type onions
½ cup roasted peanuts
4 tablesps. sour cream
Salt and red pepper, to taste
1 tablesp. oil
4 tablesps. tomato juice

1. Parboil onions for 10 minutes; drain. Peel, and remove part of centers.

2. Chop pulp and peanuts, mix with sour cream and season.

3. Fill onions with mixture and place in shallow baking dish.

4. Sprinkle with oil, add tomato juice, and bake, uncovered, in moderate oven for about 20 minutes.

STUFFED ONIONS

4 large flat onions	plain yogurt
1 dill pickle or canned pimiento	Salt, marjoram and red pepper, to taste
1 slice stale rye bread	¼ cup vegetable stock, or water
3 to 4 tablesps. sour cream or	

1. Cook onions whole; drain and cool.

2. Remove part of centers; chop pulp together with dill pickle or pimiento.

3. Grate bread and mix with chopped onion.

4. Blend well with sour cream, and season. Stuff onion with mixture.

5. Place in baking dish with vegetable stock or water, cover, and bake in a moderate oven for 10 minutes. Uncover, baste if necessary, and bake for additional 10 minutes.

FRIED PARSNIPS

4 medium parsnips	Salt, nutmeg and white pepper, to taste
1 clove garlic	Chopped chives or parsley
3 tablesps. oil	
2 tablesps. sour cream	

1. Cook and drain parsnips; peel; slice.

2. Rub pan with cut clove of garlic and salt.

3. Pan parsnips in hot oil over a low flame for 5 minutes.

4. Season sour cream and pour over parsnips; mix lightly, cover, and simmer for 10 minutes.

5. Sprinkle with chives or parsley, and serve.

MASHED PARSNIPS WITH ONION RINGS

4 medium parsnips	5 tablesps. oil
1 large onion	Salt and red pepper, to taste

1. Cook parsnips, drain, peel and mash.

2. Slice onion into rings and pan in 2 tablesps. oil until golden brown; reserve.

3. Heat remaining oil, add to mashed parsnips, season, and with fork or egg beater, beat parsnips until light and fluffy. Keep hot.

4. Garnish parsnips with onion rings, and serve.

NUTTY PARSNIP FRITTERS

4 medium parsnips	Oil for deep frying
½ cup chopped roasted peanuts	Salt, red pepper or nutmeg, to taste
French pancake batter	Chopped chives

1. Cook and drain parsnips and remove skins; if young, cut in halves, otherwise slice finger-thick.

2. Roll parsnips in nuts, dip in batter, and deep-fry in hot oil until golden brown.

3. Drain on paper, sprinkle with seasoning and chives, and serve.

PEAS—MEXICAN STYLE

1 fresh pimiento or 2 canned
1 large tomato
2 tablesps. oil or pimiento oil
   from can
3 cups peas, cooked fresh or
   frozen

Salt, onion salt and white
   pepper, to taste
1 teasp. flour

1. Chop pimiento; slice or cut tomato into quarters.
2. Pan pimiento in hot oil for 5 minutes.
3. Add peas, season, cover, and simmer for 5 minutes.
4. Stir in flour and let come to a quick boil.

PEA GOULASH

4 to 6 mushrooms
3 large fresh tomatoes or
   1 ½ cups stewed
1 medium onion
4 slices stale rye bread
3 tablesps. oil
3 cups drained peas, cooked

fresh or frozen
1 teasp. brown sugar
Salt and paprika, to taste
About ½ cup vegetable
   stock, or water
2 to 3 tablesps. sherry

1. Quarter mushrooms; slice or cut tomatoes in quarters; slice onion; cube bread.
2. Pan onion and mushrooms in 2 tablesps. hot oil for 5 minutes.
3. Add peas, tomatoes, sugar and seasoning; moisten with a few tablesps. of stock, if necessary; cover and simmer over a low flame for 5 minutes.
4. Add wine and simmer, uncovered, for additional 5 minutes.
5. Heat remaining oil and fry bread until crisp.
6. Turn out on serving dish, sprinkle with bread croutons, and serve.

PEAS WITH RICE

1 ½ cups cooked brown rice
2 ½ cups peas, cooked fresh
or frozen
2 tablesps. oil
Salt and paprika, to taste

Dash of saffron or curry
4 tablesps. grated cheese,
preferably Parmesan
type

1. Mix rice and peas and heat thoroughly over a low flame.

2. Add oil and seasonings and blend well.

3. Turn out on serving dish, sprinkle with cheese, and serve.

UNSHELLED PEAS WITH BUTTER SAUCE

2 pounds very young green
peas
3 to 4 cups vegetable stock,
or water

1 teasp. brown sugar
6 tablesps. butter
1 tablesp. lemon juice
Chopped parsley

1. Drop unshelled peas into boiling vegetable stock, add sugar, cover, and simmer until shells are tender. Drain and turn into vegetable dish; keep warm.

2. Heat butter, add lemon juice and parsley, cook over a low flame until butter turns light brown, and pour into sauce dish.

To eat: Dip each shell into butter sauce.

SPANISH RISOTTO

About 4 cups vegetable stock,
or water
1 cup rice
2 to 3 canned pimientos
1 green pepper
½ pound mushrooms
4 tablesps. oil

Salt and cayenne pepper, to
taste
2 cups peas, cooked fresh or
frozen
Grated cheese, Parmesan
type

1. Keep vegetable stock hot over a low flame until used.

2. Clean but do not wash rice.

3. Slice or chop pimientos, pepper and mushrooms, and pan in hot oil for about 5 minutes; season.

4. Add rice and brown for 5 minutes, stirring constantly. Add 4 to 5 tablesps. hot liquid and stir with a wooden spoon until liquid is absorbed. Repeat, stirring constantly and adding liquid each time rice becomes dry. Risotto is ready when it has been stirred for 18 minutes.

5. Remove from flame, add peas, and mix well.

6. Turn out on serving dish and serve, with cheese in a separate dish.

GREEN PEPPER AND TOMATO CASSEROLE

4 to 5 medium peppers	Salt, nutmeg, basil or marjoram, to taste
3 large fresh tomatoes or 1 ½ cups stewed	½ cup sour cream or plain yogurt
1 clove garlic	
2 tablesps. oil	2 tablesps tomato juice

1. Cover peppers with boiling water and allow to stand for 3 minutes. Cut off stem end, remove seeds, and cut into finger-thick strips.

2. Quarter or slice tomatoes.

3. Rub saucepan with cut clove of garlic and salt; heat oil in pan, and pan peppers, covered, over a very low flame for 10 minutes.

4. Season peppers, add tomatoes and cream, cover and simmer for 10 minutes. If stewed tomatoes are used, cook only 5 minutes.

5. Turn out on serving dish, pour tomato juice over top, and serve.

BROILED GREEN PEPPERS

5 medium green peppers	Salt, to taste
2 tablesps. oil	Pinch of cayenne pepper
3 hard-cooked eggs	½ cup milk
1 tablesp. flour	

1. Cover peppers with boiling water and let stand for 3 minutes. Cut off stem end, remove seeds, and cut into fine strips.

2. Pan peppers in hot oil over a low flame for 10 minutes, stirring occasionally.

3. Slice hard-cooked eggs; blend flour and seasonings into milk.

4. Turn peppers into shallow baking dish, cover with sliced eggs, and pour milk and flour mixture over it.

5. Place under medium broiler for about 15 minutes or until most of the liquid has disappeared and top is brown.

STUFFED GREEN PEPPERS

4 large green peppers	1 ½ cups tomato juice
Stuffing	

1. Cut off stem end, remove seeds, put into boiling water, cover, and let stand for 2 minutes. Drain and cool.

2. Fill with desired stuffing.

3. Place stuffed peppers in baking dish, pour in tomato juice and bake, covered, in a moderate oven for 10 to 15 minutes. Uncover, and bake another 5 minutes.

4. Serve in baking dish.

STUFFINGS

Rice and Mushroom Stuffing: Mix 2 cups cooked rice with ¼ pound panned mushrooms, 1 chopped hard-cooked egg, and ½ teasp. prepared mustard; season with salt and chopped parsley.

Corn Stuffing: Mix 2 cups cooked kernel corn with 4 tablesps. grated cheese, and moisten mixture with 1 or 2 tablesps. milk or cream; season with salt and chopped parsley, or red pepper.

Potato Stuffing: Mix 2 cups cooked diced potatoes with ½ tablesp. caraway seeds and blend well with ½ teasp. Worcestershire or soy sauce, or onion juice.

Cauliflower Stuffing: Mix 1 cup cooked cauliflower, broken into flowerets, with 1 cup cheese sauce, and season to taste.

Spicy Stuffing: Mix ½ pound cottage cheese with 2 chopped canned pimientos, and 8 to 10 pitted and chopped black olives. Season with nutmeg and paprika.

Soybean Stuffing: Mix 1 ½ cups cooked soybeans (either dried or fresh green) with 1 tablesp. tomato paste, 4 tablesps. cottage cheese, and salt and paprika, to taste.

AUSTRIAN BAKED POTATOES

1 ½ pounds small potatoes   4 to 5 tablesps. oil
1 medium onion   Salt and marjoram, to taste

1. Slice unpeeled potatoes into thin slices; chop or slice onion.

2. Place potatoes and onions in a shallow baking dish, dot with oil and sprinkle with salt and marjoram.

3. Bake, uncovered, in a moderate oven for about 35 minutes or until tender.

4. Serve immediately.

BREADED POTATO BALLS

1 ½ pounds medium   6 tablesps. oil
   potatoes   Salt, to taste
1 bay leaf   ½ cup bread or cracker
2 hard-cooked eggs   crumbs
2 egg whites

1. Cook unpeeled potatoes with bay leaf.

2. Chop eggs; beat egg whites stiff but not dry.

3. Peel and rice potatoes, mix immediately with 4 tablesps. oil and salt, and cut and fold in egg whites.

4. Pan bread crumbs in remaining oil until golden brown; mix with chopped eggs.

5. Shape potato mixture into balls, roll in bread crumb mixture, and serve immediately on a warm platter. If vegetable is too cool, set balls on a baking sheet and heat in a moderate oven for about 10 minutes.

FRIED POTATO CAKES

4 medium potatoes   Salt and paprika, to taste
1 large onion   2 to 3 tablesps. oil
Juice of ½ lemon

1. Shred unpeeled potatoes on a coarse shredder.

2. Chop onion fine and mix with potatoes; add lemon juice and seasoning, and blend well.

3. Heat oil in heavy skillet, drop mixture by the spoonful into the oil, flatten each immediately into a thin cake, and fry on both sides until golden brown, turning only once.

4. Serve immediately on a warm platter.

HUNGARIAN POTATOES

6 medium potatoes (about 1 ½ pounds)	Flour
1 green pepper	4 tablesps. oil
2 large ripe tomatoes or 1 cup stewed	1 teasp. caraway seeds
	Salt and paprika, to taste

1. Parboil potatoes for 10 minutes; peel and cut in ½-inch slices.

2. Chop pepper, and slice or cut up tomatoes.

3. Dredge potato slices in flour, and pan in hot oil for 3 minutes.

4. Add tomatoes, pepper, caraway seeds, and season. Cover and cook over a low flame for 15 minutes or until potatoes are tender.

NEW POTATOES

1 ½ pounds new potatoes	Chopped chives or dill or
2 to 3 tablesps. butter or oil	parsley or caraway seeds
Salt, to taste	

1. Cook potatoes in skin.

2. Melt butter, sprinkle with salt, add chopped parsley, dill, chives, or caraway seeds; add peeled potatoes, roll about to coat well, and serve.

PEASANT OMELETTE

4 large potatoes	Salt and paprika, to taste
1 green pepper or pickle	4 eggs
3 tablesps. oil	2 to 3 tablesps. milk

1. Cook potatoes.

2. Chop pepper or pickle, and peel and dice or slice potatoes.

3. Add to hot oil, season, cover, and pan for 10 minutes, stirring occasionally.

4. Blend eggs with milk, pour over potatoes, and cook until eggs are set.

Serve immediately.

POTATO AND SPINACH FRITTERS

1 pound potatoes	marjoram, to taste
1 cup cooked chopped spinach	Drop batter
	Oil for deep frying
Salt and black pepper or	

1. Cook, peel and mash potatoes.

2. Mix potatoes, well-drained spinach, and seasoning.

3. Shape into fritters, dip in batter, and deep-fry in hot oil until golden brown.

4. Drain and serve.

POTATOES AU GRATIN

1 ½ pounds small potatoes	3 cups milk, or half milk, half water
2 hard-cooked eggs	
6 black olives	4 tablesps. grated cheese
Chopped parsley	2 tablesps. oil
Salt, to taste	

1. Cook potatoes; peel and slice.

2. Slice eggs; pit and chop olives.

3. Line the bottom of a well-greased baking dish with half of potatoes; cover with eggs, sprinkle with olives, parsley and salt. Cover with remaining potatoes.

4. Mix milk with cheese and pour over potatoes; sprinkle with oil.

5. Bake, uncovered, in a moderate oven for about 30 minutes or until golden brown. Serve soon.

POTATO RAMEKINS

4 medium potatoes	Salt and paprika, to taste
3 eggs	Chopped parsley
4 to 5 large mushrooms	½ cup grated cheese
2 tablesps. oil	

1. Cook and peel potatoes; mash or rice.

2. Separate eggs and beat yolks until light and creamy; beat whites stiff but not dry.

3. Slice mushrooms and pan in hot oil over a very low flame for 5 minutes.

4. Mix potatoes with egg yolks, season, and cut and fold in egg whites. Put into individual greased baking dishes or custard cups. Sprinkle with parsley.

5. Cover with mushrooms and top with cheese.

6. Place under moderate broiler, and broil for 10 minutes or until cheese is melted and top brown.

POTATO RING

1 ½ pounds potatoes	3 tablesps. oil
Salt and white pepper, to taste	1 cup milk
	1 ½ cups sauce (choice)
2 eggs	

1. Cook potatoes; peel and mash. Season.

2. Separate eggs; beat yolks until light, whites until stiff but not dry.

3. Add the oil, milk and egg yolks to hot potatoes and cream until fluffy; cut and fold in egg whites.

4. Put in buttered ring mold, set in a pan of hot water, and bake in a moderate oven for about 15 minutes.

5. Unmold, cover with sauce (cheese, horseradish, or tomato), and serve.

POTATO SOUFFLE

1 ½ pounds potatoes
2 egg whites
6 tablesps. butter

Salt and marjoram, to taste
½ cup grated cheese

1. Cook potatoes.
2. Beat egg whites stiff but not dry.
3. Mash potatoes, add 3 tablesps. butter and seasoning, mix well, and cut and fold in egg whites.
4. Place in a greased shallow baking dish, cover with cheese and dot with remaining butter.
5. Bake, uncovered, in a moderate oven for 15 minutes, and serve immediately.

POTATOES WITH SAUERKRAUT

6 medium potatoes (about
    1 ½ pounds)
1 ½ cups sauerkraut

2 cups vegetable stock, or
    water
1 cup tomato juice
4 to 6 tablesps. grated cheese

1. Scrape or peel potatoes and cut in halves.
2. Mix sauerkraut with vegetable stock and tomato juice; distribute potatoes evenly in the sauerkraut. Cover and simmer for about 30 minutes or until vegetables are tender.
3. Sprinkle with cheese, and serve.

PUFFED BAKED POTATOES

4 medium baking potatoes
1 tablesp. oil
Salt, to taste

1 teasp. chopped caraway
    seeds

1. Cut washed, dried potatoes in half lengthwise, and place, cut side down, on a well-greased baking sheets.
2. Rub skin well with oil and sprinkle with salt and caraway seeds.

3. Bake in a hot oven until potatoes are tender and puffed up (20 to 30 minutes depending on size of potatoes).

Serve immediately.

STUFFED BAKED POTATOES

2 large or 4 small Idaho potatoes	1 tablesp. milk or cream
Oil	Stuffing (choice)
	Chopped dill or chives

1. Rub potatoes lightly with oil, and bake.

2. When ready, cut lengthwise into halves, if large; if small, cut thin slice off from flat end; scoop out.

3. Blend scooped-out potato with milk or cream, and mix with stuffing.

4. Fill skins with mixture and put back in oven to heat.

5. Sprinkle with dill or chives and serve.

STUFFINGS

Sauerkraut Stuffing: 4 tablesps. sauerkraut, 1 teasp. chopped caraway seeds, no salt, but pepper or paprika, to taste.

Peanut Stuffing: 4 tablesps. chopped peanuts and 1 tablesp. oil; paprika and onion juice, to taste.

Cottage Cheese Stuffing: 4 tablesps. cottage cheese, 1 tablesp. milk, and seasoning to taste.

Mushroom Stuffing: ¼ pound mushrooms, sliced and panned in 1 tablesp. oil, salt and pepper for seasoning.

Spinach Stuffing: ½ cup cooked, drained spinach or other greens, chopped, mixed with 1 tablesp. oil; and salt and pepper for seasoning.

Onion Stuffing: ½ cup cooked onions, or 1 to 2 leeks, or 8 to 10 scallions, panned; salt and pepper, to taste.

Olive Stuffing: 12 black or green olives, and 1 canned
pimiento, chopped, and 2 to 3 tablesps. cracker
crumbs.

SMOTHERED RADISHES

2 bunches radishes, red or white   Salt and pepper, to taste
Flour   1 tablesp. white wine, if
1 cup light cream   desired
½ cup tomato juice

1. Scrape radishes, if white are used. Dredge well
with flour.

2. Mix cream and tomato juice and heat; add radishes
and remaining ingredients. Cover and simmer for 10
to 15 minutes or until radishes are tender.

Serve immediately.

ROMAINE AU GRATIN

2 medium heads romaine   Salt and savory, to taste
1 large onion   ½ cup grated cheese or 4
2 tablesps. oil   tablesps. cottage cheese
½ cup cream, sour or sweet   Chopped parsley

1. Thoroughly dry romaine after washing. Cut small
leaves in half lengthwise, large leaves in half both
lengthwise and crosswise, and place in greased baking
dish.

2. Chop onion and pan in hot oil for about 5 minutes

3. Mix with cream and season, pour mixture over
romaine, sprinkle with grated cheese or crumbled cottage cheese.

4. Bake, covered, in a moderate oven for 20 minutes.
Uncover and bake for additional 10 minutes.

5. Sprinkle with parsley and serve.

BRAISED ROMAINE OR HEAD LETTUCE

4 small or 2 medium heads   4 tablesps. oil
   romaine or head lettuce   Salt and marjoram, to taste
4 tablesps. tomato paste   1 tablesp. lemon juice

1. Wash vegetable thoroughly. Tie each head separately with string, place in saucepan, add enough water to barely cover, and simmer, covered, over a low flame for 5 minutes. Drain, if necessary, and remove strings. Place vegetable in shallow baking dish.

2. Cream tomato paste with oil and seasoning, spread over vegetable and broil under medium broiler for 10 to 15 minutes.

3. Sprinkle with lemon juice, and serve.

MOCK ASPARAGUS (ROMAINE)

4 small or 2 medium heads   3 tablesps. oil
   romaine   4 to 5 tablesps. bread or
about 2 cups vegetable stock,   cracker crumbs
   or water   Lemon juice
Salt and white pepper, to
   taste

1. Separate romaine into leaves; using several leaves roll into cigar-like rolls; tie each roll with cord.

2. Barely cover with liquid and cook for 10 minutes or until tender. Drain, and season.

3. Heat oil and fry crumbs until golden brown.

4. Turn vegetable out on serving dish, remove cord, cover one end with bread crumbs, sprinkle vegetable with lemon juice, and serve.

RUTABAGAS (YELLOW TURNIPS)—SWEDISH STYLE

2 pounds rutabagas   1 cup milk
2 large onions   Salt and black pepper, to
3 to 4 tablesps. oil   taste

1. Cook rutabagas until tender and drain.
2. Slice onions into rings and pan in hot oil until light brown; keep warm.
3. Mash rutabagas, mix with hot milk, season, and turn into serving dish.
4. Cover with onion rings and oil, and serve.

See also recipes for Turnips.

SALSIFY (OYSTERPLANT) AU GRATIN

6 to 8 salsify roots
1 tablesp. flour and ½ cup tomato juice
    or
½ cup sour cream or

plain yogurt
Salt, red pepper and nutmeg to taste
3 to 4 tablesps. grated cheese
1 tablesp. oil

1. Cook salsify, drain, and cut in 2-inch pieces.
2. Blend flour and tomato juice and season, or season sour cream.
3. Place salsify in well-greased shallow baking dish, cover with tomato juice or sour cream, sprinkle with cheese and oil, and bake, uncovered, in a moderate oven for 15 to 20 minutes. Or broil under medium flame for about 15 minutes or until cheese is melted and top brown.

SALSIFY (OYSTERPLANT)—DUTCH STYLE

6 to 8 salsify roots
2 tablesps. bread or cracker crumbs

2 tablesps. oil
3 tablesps. grated cheese
Salt and paprika, to taste

1. Cook salsify, drain and cut into 2-inch pieces.
2. Fry bread crumbs in hot oil until golden brown, add salsify, shake well and leave on a very low flame until vegetable is thoroughly hot.
3. Sprinkle with grated cheese, season and serve.
A well-seasoned mayonnaise or hot sauce goes well with this dish.

SALSIFY (OYSTERPLANT) FRITTERS

6 to 8 salsify roots   Oil for deep frying
Salt and nutmeg, to taste   Lemon slices
French pancake batter   Sprigs of parsley

1. Cook salsify, drain, cut in halves crosswise, and season.

2. Dip in batter and deep-fry in hot oil until golden brown.

3. Drain on paper, garnish with lemon slices and parsley, and serve.

MOCK OYSTERS (SALSIFY)

8 salsify roots   Salt and paprika, to taste
1 tablesp. cream   Oil for frying
1 egg   Lemon slices
Dash of red wine, if desired   Tabasco sauce

1. Cook salsify, drain and mash. Mix with cream and well-beaten egg; add wine and season.

2. Shape into oyster-sized patties and fry in hot oil until golden brown. Turn only once.

3. Garnish with lemon slices and serve with Tabasco sauce.

BAKED SAUERKRAUT WITH APPLES

3 medium potatoes   1 teasp. paprika
3 medium apples   ½ teasp. nutmeg
1 medium onion   4 tablesps. cracker crumbs
2 cups sauerkraut   1 to 2 tablesps. oil

1. Cook and mash or slice potatoes.

2. Core and shred unpeeled apples; chop onion; blend well.

3. Grease baking dish, and fill with alternate layers of sauerkraut, potatoes and apples. Start with sauerkraut and make top layer sauerkraut.

4. Season each layer with paprika and nutmeg, and sprinkle top with crumbs and oil.

5. Cover and bake in a moderate oven for about 30 minutes; uncover, and bake for another 10 minutes.

BAKED EGGS IN SAUERKRAUT

1 green pepper
2 cups sauerkraut
1 teasp. caraway seeds

2 tablesps. tomato juice
4 eggs
Salt, to taste

1. Chop green pepper.

2. Mix sauerkraut, pepper, caraway seeds and tomato juice, and place in shallow baking dish. Form 4 nests to hold eggs.

3. Break eggs into nests and sprinkle with salt.

4. Bake in a moderate oven until eggs are set and sauerkraut is tender (about 30 minutes).

STEAMED SAUERKRAUT—HUNGARIAN STYLE

4 to 5 ripe tomatoes or
    1 ½ cups stewed
3 tablesps. oil
4 cups sauerkraut (about 1
    pound)

1 tablesp. caraway seeds
½ cup vegetable stock, if
    necessary

1. Cut tomatoes into quarters.

2. Heat oil, add sauerkraut, tomatoes and caraway seeds, and pan for 5 minutes. Add vegetable stock, if necessary; cover and simmer for 20 minutes or until tender.

HOME-MADE FRESH SAUERKRAUT

10 pounds white cabbage
4 to 5 medium apples
2 large lemons
1 tablesp. juniper berries

1 tablesp. caraway seeds
1 quart water, boiled and
    cooled to 95° F.

1. Shred cabbage and pound well; core and slice unpeeled apples; slice lemons.

2. Place layers of cabbage in bottom of a crock, cover with a thin layer of apples, lemons and spices. Repeat layers until all the cabbage is used up. Top layer must be cabbage.

3. When cabbage is in crock pound thoroughly again, in order to squeeze out the air.

4. Cover with water, let settle, cover with a *linen* cloth and a plate. Weight with a heavy stone.

5. Keep in a cool place. If after three days the cabbage is not completely covered by liquid, add water which has been boiled and cooled to 95° F.

This sauerkraut is flavorful and is without the usual salty taste. As it will not keep more than 3 weeks, prepare only the quantity indicated in the recipe and use up in that time.

SPINACH AND CHEESE SOUFFLÉ

2 pounds spinach	1 cup milk
1 teasp. oil	2 tablesps. sour cream
Salt and nutmeg, to taste	4 eggs
1 tablesp. flour	4 tablesps. grated cheese

1. Cook spinach, drain, and chop very fine.

2. Heat oil, add spinach, salt and nutmeg, and pan for 5 minutes, stir in flour; mix well, avoiding lumps. Add milk and sour cream gradually; and let come to a quick boil. Cool.

3. Separate eggs, beat egg whites stiff but not dry, and mix with 2 tablesps. cheese.

4. Stir egg yolks into cooled spinach and cut and fold in egg whites.

5. Turn into well-greased baking dish, sprinkle with remaining cheese, set in a pan of hot water, and bake in a moderate oven for 25 minutes. Serve immediately.

SPINACH BALLS

4 medium potatoes
1 pound spinach
¼ teasp. dry mustard
Dash of cayenne pepper
Salt and red pepper, to taste

1 egg
Flour, if needed
3 tablesps. butter or oil
Chopped peanuts

1. Cook, peel, and rice potatoes; chop raw spinach.
2. Stir spinach into potatoes, season, and mix well.
3. Stir in well-beaten egg and thicken with flour, if too thin to handle easily.
4. Form into balls, drop into boiling salted water, cover, and simmer for 10 minutes or until firm.
5. Drop spinach balls into melted butter and shake until well-coated. Sprinkle with peanuts, and serve.

SPINACH CASSEROLE

2 pounds spinach
1 medium onion
1 medium carrot or 3 red
   radishes
Salt and mace, to taste
1 cup sour cream or

plain yogurt
1 tablesp. tomato paste
2 eggs
½ cup bread crumbs
1 teasp. oil

1. Cook and drain spinach, and chop coarsely; grate or chop onion and carrot or radishes, mix well, and season.
2. Mix sour cream and tomato paste with well-beaten eggs, add spinach mixture, and mix thoroughly.
3. Pour into well-greased baking dish, cover with bread crumbs, sprinkle with oil, and bake in a moderate oven for about 20 minutes.

SPINACH ROLL

1 pound spinach	plain yogurt
3 eggs	1 to 2 tablesps. flour
Salt and nutmeg, to taste	Chopped chives or dill
½ cup sour cream or	

1. Drain and chop raw spinach very fine or put through the food chopper.

2. Separate eggs; beat yolks until light, whites until stiff but not dry.

3. Mix egg yolks with spinach, seasoning, sour cream, and 1 or 2 tablesps. flour; blend well. Cut and fold in egg whites.

4. Pour mixture in a well-greased shallow baking dish, and bake, uncovered, in a moderate oven for about 20 minutes.

5. Sprinkle with chopped chives or dill, and roll immediately.

6. Serve on a warm platter.

BAKED SQUASH SLICES

2 pounds summer squash	Salt and paprika, to taste
1 clove garlic	2 tablesps. oil
Flour	

1. Slice squash, rub with cut clove of garlic, and dredge in flour.

2. Place on an ungreased baking sheet, sprinkle with seasoning and oil.

3. Bake in a moderate oven for about 15 minutes or until tender. Serve soon.

FRENCH - FRIED SQUASH

2 pounds summer squash	Salt, red pepper and marjoram, to taste
French pancake batter	
Oil for deep frying	

1. Slice squash and dip slices into batter until well coated.

2. Drop into hot oil and fry until golden brown.

3. Drain on paper, season, and serve.

PANNED SQUASH

2 pounds summer squash	Flour
Salt and marjoram, to taste	4 to 6 tablesps. oil
Dash of cayenne pepper	Chopped parsley

1. Peel squash only if skin is tough; cut into ½-inch slices, sprinkle with seasoning and dredge in flour.

2. Pan in hot oil until golden brown, turning only once.

3. Turn out on a warm platter, sprinkle with parsley, and serve.

SQUASH IN CREAM

2 pounds summer squash	½ cup cream, sweet or sour
Flour	4 tablesps. tomato juice
4 tablesps. oil	Chopped parsley or dill
Salt and paprika, to taste	

1. Slice or cube squash; dredge in flour and pan in hot oil until slightly brown (2 to 3 minutes); season.

2. Mix cream, tomato juice, and parsley or dill.

3. Place squash in well-greased baking dish, cover with cream and tomato mixture, and bake, uncovered, in a moderate oven for 10 to 15 minutes.

SQUASH—HUNGARIAN STYLE

3 pounds summer squash	Salt and nutmeg, to taste
3 large ripe tomatoes or 1 ½ cups stewed	1 bay leaf
2 green peppers	½ cup kernel corn, cooked fresh or frozen
½ pound mushrooms	1 teasp. brown sugar
1 tablesp. chopped parsley	½ cup sour cream
3 tablesps. oil or butter	1 teasp. cornstarch, if necessary

1. Peel squash only if skin is tough; dice squash and tomatoes. Slice or chop green peppers and mushrooms.

2. Pan parsley in hot oil for 3 minutes; add squash, and pan for another 5 minutes; add tomatoes, peppers, mushrooms, seasoning and bay leaf. Cover, and simmer over a low flame for 10 minutes.

3. Remove bay leaf; add corn, cover and simmer for an additional 5 minutes. Add sugar and cream, stir well; if watery, thicken with cornstarch; let come to a quick boil, and serve.

HUBBARD SQUASH FRITTERS

1 cooked potato	1 egg
3 to 4 cups cooked, mashed Hubbard squash	3 to 4 tablesps bread or cracker crumbs
Salt and red pepper or savory or sage, to taste	Oil for frying

1. Mash potato and mix with squash and seasoning.

2. Add well-beaten egg and blend again.

3. Shape into fritters, roll in bread or cracker crumbs, and fry in hot oil on both sides until golden brown. Turn only once.

Serve immediately.

HUBBARD SQUASH—RUSSIAN STYLE

1 medium onion	1 teasp. sugar
4 to 5 sprigs dill	Salt and black pepper, to taste
1 tablesp. oil	
4 cups cooked, cubed Hubbard squash	1 tablesp. vinegar or lemon juice, if desired
½ cup sour cream	

1. Chop or slice onion; chop dill.

2. Pan onion in hot oil until tender; add squash, and pan for 3 minutes.

3. Mix sour cream with dill, sugar and seasoning; add lemon juice or vinegar, if a very sour taste is desired.

4. Mix with squash, and simmer, covered, for 5 minutes.

HUBBARD SQUASH CUSTARD

2 eggs
½ cup milk
2 cups cooked, mashed Hubbard squash
Salt, caraway seeds and pepper, to taste
2 tablesps. bread or cracker crumbs
2 tablesps. oil
Chopped chives or dill

1. Beat eggs until light and blend well with milk.

2. Add squash and seasoning, and blend.

3. Place in well-greased baking dish, sprinkle with crumbs and dot with oil.

4. Set in a pan of hot water, and bake in a moderate oven until set. To test, insert knife, and if it comes out clean, custard is set.

5. Sprinkle with chives or dill, and serve.

SWEET POTATOES IN MADEIRA SAUCE

4 medium sweet potatoes
1 cup Madeira sauce
1 tablesp. honey

1. Cook, peel, and rice potatoes.

2. Mix with sauce and honey, and beat until light.

3. Pile lightly in shallow baking dish and broil under medium heat for about 10 minutes.

SWEET POTATOES WITH CUMBERLAND SAUCE

4 medium sweet potatoes
1 cup Cumberland sauce

8 cloves
6 marshmallows

1. Boil, peel and cut potatoes in halves lengthwise; scoop out.

2. Mix potato with Cumberland sauce and fill skins.

3. Place in shallow baking dish, stick clove in center of each stuffed shell, and dot with bits of marshmallow.

4. Broil under medium broiler until marshmallow melts.

SWEET POTATOES WITH PINEAPPLE

4 medium sweet potatoes
½ cup drained crushed
  pineapple

Cinnamon and nutmeg, to
  taste
1 tablesp. butter
½ cup brown sugar

1. Cook, peel and rice potatoes; mix well with pineapple and seasoning.

2. Place in well-greased baking dish, dot with butter and scatter sugar over it evenly.

3. Bake in a hot oven until sugar has melted (about 15 minutes).

BAKED TOMATOES WITH CHEESE

1 green pepper
½ cup sour cream
1 teasp. flour
6 thin slices bread
2 cups cut up tomatoes,
  fresh or stewed

Salt, to taste
Chopped parsley or dill
¼ pound mild cheese, cut
  into slivers
2 tablesps. oil

1. Shred pepper; blend sour cream with flour.

2. Grease baking dish, place 2 slices bread on bottom, a layer of tomatoes and pepper, sprinkle with salt and

parsley or dill, and a layer of cheese. Repeat twice, making top layer bread.

3. Pour cream mixture over top, sprinkle with oil, and bake, uncovered, in a moderate oven for about 30 minutes.

BAKED TOMATOES WITH PEANUTS

3 cups cut up tomatoes,
    fresh or stewed
1 cup chopped peanuts

Chopped parsley
Paprika, to taste
1 tablesp. oil

1. Mix tomatoes with peanuts, and place in well-greased shallow baking dish. Sprinkle with parsley, paprika and oil.

2. Bake, uncovered, in a moderate oven for 10 to 15 minutes.

BROILED TOMATOES

4 firm tomatoes
Salt, to taste
2 slices stale rye bread
2 tablesps. sour cream or

plain yogurt
8 slices thin toast
Parsley sprigs

1. Cut tomatoes into halves and sprinkle with salt.
2. Grate bread and mix with sour cream.
3. Place tomatoes, cut side up, in a greased shallow baking dish, and cover each half with ½ tablesp. sour cream mixture.
4. Broil under medium broiler for about 10 minutes or until tender and browned.
5. Serve on toast, garnished with parsley.

FRENCH-FRIED TOMATOES

4 very firm tomatoes
Drop batter

Oil for deep frying
Salt and pepper, to taste

1. Slice tomatoes.
2. Dip into batter until well coated.
3. Drop into hot oil and fry until golden brown.
4. Drain on paper, sprinkle with salt and pepper, and serve.

SPICY TOMATO STEW

1 pound fresh tomatoes or 2 cups stewed	½ cup kernel corn, cooked fresh or frozen
1 medium onion	Salt and red pepper, to taste
1 medium apple	1 tablesp. horseradish
2 tablesps. oil	

1. Cut up tomatoes, chop onion and cored, unpeeled apple.
2. Heat oil and add all ingredients except horseradish, cover, and simmer for 15 minutes; less, if stewed tomatoes are used. Season.
3. Turn out on warm serving dish, sprinkle with horseradish, and serve.

STUFFED TOMATOES

4 large tomatoes	3 tablesp. butter or oil
Stuffing	

1. Cut off stem end and scoop out inside, leaving a ½-inch thick shell.
2. Fill with desired stuffing.
3. Place stuffed tomatoes in well-greased baking dish, dot with butter, and bake, uncovered, for 20 minutes.
Serve in baking dish.
NOTE: Use left-over pulp for making soups or sauces, or in stews.
STUFFINGS
(If quantity in the following recipes is insufficient to stuff tomatoes well, use more of any or all of the ingredients in each recipe, or tomato pulp.)

Nutmeat Stuffing: Mix 4 tablesps. each of chopped nutmeats, tomato pulp, and cottage cheese; season with salt and chopped parsley.

Lima Bean Stuffing: Mix ½ cup cooked beans with 4 tablesps. cheese sauce or white sauce; season with salt and nutmeg.

Rice and Mushroom Stuffing: Mix ½ cup cooked rice, 1 medium chopped green pepper, and ¼ pound sliced, panned mushrooms, with 2 tablesps. each of milk and grated cheese; season with salt and paprika.

Mixed Vegetable Stuffing: Mix 4 tablesps. each of spinach, mashed potatoes, and tomato pulp, and season with salt and marjoram; or, mix ¾ cup cabbage with 2 tablesps. sour cream and chopped olives; or, chop ½ cup sauerkraut, mix with 4 tablesps. riced potatoes, and season with paprika.

Spicy Corn Stuffing: Mix ½ cup cooked corn with 1 or 2 chopped (canned) pimientos and chopped tomato pulp; add salt to taste.

Poached Egg Stuffing: Drop one raw egg into each tomato shell, sprinkle with grated cheese and season with salt and paprika. If tomato cups are large, cover bottom with chopped onions mixed with pulp and panned, before dropping in eggs.

TOMATO DIUVEC

2 green peppers
1 medium onion
1 hard-cooked egg
½ clove garlic
2 ½ cups cut up tomatoes, fresh or stewed

½ cup uncooked rice
Salt and marjoram, to taste
1 ½ cups vegetable stock, or water
3 tablesps. grated cheese
1 tablesp. oil

1. Chop peppers and onion; slice egg.

2. Rub baking dish with garlic, and grease well; put in half of tomatoes, cover with rice, and pepper and onion mixture, and top with remaining tomatoes.

3. Season liquid, pour over vegetable, cover, and bake in a moderate oven for 15 minutes.

4. Uncover, sprinkle with cheese and oil, and bake for 20 minutes.

5. Garnish with egg slices and serve.

TOMATOES—SERBIAN STYLE

1 cup brown rice	5 large ripe tomatoes or 2
4 medium onions	cups stewed
3 green peppers	3 to 4 tablesps. oil

1. Cook rice, uncovered, in 4 ½ cups water, until tender. Drain when ready, and keep warm.

2. Peel and slice onions into rings; cut peppers into strips; and cut up tomatoes.

3. Heat oil and pan onion for 2 minutes.

4. Add pepper, cover, and cook over a low flame for 5 minutes.

5. Add tomatoes and cook, uncovered, for an additional 10 minutes.

6. Place rice on platter, pour tomatoes over it, and serve.

TURNIPS AU GRATIN

2 bunches turnips (about 2 pounds)	Salt and nutmeg, to taste
1 large onion	1 ½ cups dill sauce
3 ripe tomatoes or 1 cup stewed	3 tablesps. grated cheese

1. Cook peeled turnips until tender, and slice, dice or quarter.

2. Chop onion, and cut up tomatoes.

3. Mix all ingredients except cheese, place in well-greased baking dish, sprinkle with cheese, and bake, uncovered, in a moderate oven until well browned (15 to 20 minutes).

TURNIPS IN MADEIRA SAUCE

2 bunches turnips (about 2 pounds)	Madeira sauce Salt, to taste

1. Cook peeled turnips until tender, and slice, dice or quarter.

2. Simmer in Madeira sauce over a very low flame for 10 minutes, add salt, if necessary, and serve.

TURNIP GREENS

See recipes for Greens and Spinach.

IRISH VEGETABLE STEW

1 small head white or green cabbage	4 tablesps. oil
3 small leeks	1 teasp. chopped caraway seeds
3 medium potatoes	3 to 4 cups vegetable stock, or water
3 medium tomatoes	
1 large onion	Salt, nutmeg and black pepper, to taste
3 medium carrots	
1 clove garlic	

1. Shred cabbage; slice leeks into rings; dice potatoes; cut tomatoes into quarters; slice or chop onion; slice or dice carrots.

2. Rub saucepan with garlic, heat oil, and pan leeks and onion for 5 minutes, stirring occasionally.

3. Add potatoes, carrots, caraway seeds, and enough vegetable stock to barely cover, and simmer, covered, until vegetables are tender. Season after 10 minutes' cooking.

If necessary, add more stock during cooking.

VEGETABLE AND RICE CASSEROLE

1 small cauliflower or cabbage	Salt and red pepper, to taste
2 carrots	1 large onion
1 stalk celery	5 to 6 cups vegetable stock, or water
4 tablesps. oil	½ cup chopped nutmeats, if desired
1 cup brown rice	

1. Slice, shred and dice all vegetables except onion, and pan in 3 tablesps. of hot oil for 5 minutes, stirring constantly.

2. Add rice (cleaned but not washed) and pan for another 2 minutes over a very low flame; season.

3. Turn into well-greased baking dish, add whole onion, and enough liquid to cover, sprinkle with remaining oil, and bake in a moderate oven until rice is tender (about 25 minutes).

4. Remove onion, sprinkle with nutmeats, and serve.

VEGETABLES BAKED IN MUSTARD SAUCE

3 cups cooked, diced or sliced vegetables—any of the following alone or in combination: cabbage, carrots, celery,	potatoes, tomatoes, turnips
	1 cup mustard sauce
	1 to 2 tablesps. sherry
	2 tablesps. butter or oil
	Chopped parsley

1. Mix vegetables with sauce and sherry; place in well-greased baking dish. Dot with butter.

2. Bake, uncovered, in a moderate oven for about 20 minutes.

3. Sprinkle with parsley, and serve.

VEGETABLE GOULASH

2 medium onions
2 green peppers
½ pound mushrooms
3 tablesps. oil
Salt and paprika, to taste
3 to 4 cups cooked, diced vegetables—any of the following alone or in combination: carrots, snap beans, turnips, potatoes, shredded cabbage, peas
1 cup tomato juice or 1 ½ cups stewed tomatoes
4 tablesps. sherry, if desired

1. Chop onions, peppers, mushrooms, and pan in hot oil until tender; season.

2. Mix with vegetables and tomatoes or tomato juice, add sherry if desired, and simmer, covered, until thoroughly hots.

ZUCCHINI A LA PROVENCALE

4 small zucchini
1 large onion
2 to 3 tablesps. cracker crumbs
2 tablesps. tomato paste
Salt and black pepper, to taste
½ clove garlic
2 to 3 tablesps. grated cheese, Parmesan type
4 to 6 black olives
1 tablesp. oil or butter

1. Wash and cut zucchini in halves and scoop out centers. Peel only if skin is tough.

2. Chop onion and inner part of zucchini very fine.

3. Blend with cracker crumbs, tomato paste and seasoning into a smooth paste.

4. Rub garlic with salt into a smooth paste and rub inside of zucchini halves with it.

5. Stuff with mixture, cover with cheese, and dot with halves of pitted olives and oil.

6. Place in a greased baking dish and bake, uncovered, in a moderate oven for 20 minutes. Serve soon.

ZUCCHINI AU GRATIN

3 medium zucchini
2 small pickles
2 firm tomatoes
Flour

Salt, to taste
4 tablesps. oil
4 tablesps. grated cheese
½ cup sour cream

1. Cut zucchini into fairly thick slices; chop pickles; slice tomatoes.
2. Dredge zucchini in salted flour and pan in 3 tablesps. hot oil for 5 minutes.
3. Place half of zucchini in well-greased, shallow baking dish, add pickles and half of cheese, and cover with remaining zucchini.
4. Mix sour cream with oil in pan, and pour over zucchini.
5. Cover with tomato slices, sprinkle with remaining oil and cheese, and broil under moderate broiler for about 20 minutes, or until cheese is melted and top brown.

See also recipes for Summer Squash.

Legumes (Dried Vegetables)

BAKED BEANS WITH TOMATOES

1 ½ cups dried beans (any kind)
3 large ripe tomatoes or 1 ½ cups stewed
¼ pound Cheddar cheese,
grated or cut into slivers
Salt, thyme and marjoram, to taste
½ cup light cream
2 tablesps. butter or oil

1. Cook beans and purée.
2. Cut up tomatoes.
3. Place half of bean purée in well-greased baking dish, cover with tomatoes, then with cheese, and top with remaining bean purée.
4. Pour cream over top, sprinkle with seasoning and dot with butter.
5. Bake, uncovered, in a moderate oven for 20 to 25 minutes.

BOSTON BAKED BEANS

1 quart pea beans
1 tablesp. salt
½ teasp. dry mustard
4 tablesps. brown sugar
4 tablesps. molasses or up to 1 cup according to taste
Boiling water

1. Cover beans with cold water and soak overnight.
2. Drain, cover with fresh water, and simmer until skins burst. Drain.
3. Mix salt, mustard, 3 tablesps. sugar and molasses, and add enough boiling water to cover mixture; stir until well mixed, and pour over beans. Add enough boiling water to cover beans.
4. Cover pot, and bake in a slow oven for 6 to 8 hours, adding more water to cover beans until the last hour.
5. Sprinkle with 1 tablesp. sugar; bake, uncovered, for the last hour.

CANDIED BEANS WITH NUTS AND APPLES

1 ½ cups dried beans (any kind
2 canned pimientos
2 medium apples
Salt and nutmeg, to taste

1 tablesp. brown sugar or honey
2 tablesps. chopped nutmeats
1 tablesp. butter or oil

1. Cook beans and drain; chop pimientos; core and slice or dice unpeeled apples.

2. Mix beans with pimientos and apples, and season.

3. Put into well-greased baking dish, sprinkle with sugar and nutmeats, and dot with fat.

4. Bake, uncovered, in a hot oven for 10 minutes.

SPICY BLACK BEANS WITH POACHED EGGS

1 to 1 ½ cups dried black beans
1 small onion
1 cucumber pickle
Rind of ½ lemon
1 tablesp. vinegar

1 teasp. prepared mustard
Salt, thyme and marjoram, to taste
4 eggs
1 tablesp. oil

1. Cook beans, and drain.

2. Chop onion, pickle and lemon rind; mix vinegar and mustard. Add to beans, and season; put over a very low flame to keep hot.

3. Fry or poach eggs; if eggs are poached, heat oil and stir into beans.

4. Turn beans out on serving dish, top with eggs, and serve.

LENTILS AND PRUNES IN SHERRY

1 ½ cups lentils
1 cup dried prunes
2 cloves
½ teasp. cinnamon

3 to 4 tablesps. sherry
½ tablesp. lemon juice
Salt, to taste

1. Cook lentils until tender, and drain.

2. Cover prunes with water, add cloves and cinnamon, and cook until tender. Remove cloves, pit prunes and mash with fork.

3. Mix lentils with prunes and wine, and add lemon juice and salt. Heat over a low flame until thoroughly hot.

This dish is quickly prepared when cooked lentils and prunes are at hand.

LENTILS O'BRIEN

2 canned pimientos
1 medium onion
2 tablesps. oil
3 cups cooked lentils

1 teasp. vinegar or lemon juice
Salt and paprika, to taste
1 lemon, sliced

1. Chop pimientos and onion, and pan in hot oil for 3 minutes.

2. Add lentils, and cook over a low flame until thoroughly heated; add vinegar or lemon juice, and season.

3. Garnish with lemon slices and serve.

BAKED LIMA BEANS IN MUSTARD SAUCE

3 cups cooked dried lima beans
1 cup quick mustard sauce
1 teasp. onion juice

Salt and white pepper, to taste
1 tablesp. butter or oil

1. Mix beans with sauce and onion juice; season.

2. Place in well-greased baking dish, dot with butter, and bake, uncovered, in a moderate oven for about 20 minutes. Or heat in top of double boiler and stir in butter before serving.

SPLIT PEAS AU GRATIN

2 cups cooked split peas   4 tablesps. grated cheese
1 cup hot garlic sauce   Sprigs of parsley
Salt, to taste

1. Mix peas with sauce and add salt, if necessary.

2. Put in a shallow baking dish, cover with cheese, and broil under medium broiler until cheese is melted (10 to 15 minutes).

3. Garnish with parsley, and serve.

SPLIT PEA FRITTERS

1 cup split peas   Chopped parsley
1 onion   Salt and paprika, to taste
1 tablesp. oil   Flour
1 egg   Oil for deep frying

1. Cook peas and purée.

2. Chop onion fine, pan in 1 tablesp. hot oil until golden brown, and stir into pea purée.

3. Add beaten egg and parsley; season and mix well.

4. Shape into fritters and dredge in flour.

5. Deep-fry in hot oil until crisp and brown. Drain on paper. Serve immediately.

SOYBEAN HASH

3 cups cooked dried soy-   Salt and red pepper, to taste
    beans   ½ cup vegetable stock, or
1 large onion   water
1 canned pimiento   2 to 3 tablesps. oil
1 cup cubed, cooked potatoes   Chopped parsley or chives

1. Chop soybeans, onion and pimiento.

2. Mix with potato, season and moisten with liquid.

3. Heat oil in heavy skillet and turn hash into it. Cook over a low flame for about 30 minutes, turning only once. When both sides are nicely brown, turn out on platter, sprinkle with parsley or chives, and serve.

SOUPS

THE SKY is the limit for vegetable combinations which can go into the making of a delicious soup. For that reason, soup is one of the very best ways to use all bits of leftover raw and cooked vegetables. An important rule for non-vegetarians to observe is that only water or vegetable stock (never a meat stock) must be used for the preparation of vegetable soups.

The following recipe for soup stock is for a vegetable stock, not for a soup; it is to be used for making soups or whenever liquid is called for in the recipes of this book. The four basic soup recipes with their many variations will serve as a scaffolding for a wide variety of healthful and economical soups to *your taste*.

VEGETABLE STOCK

3 to 4 cups raw vegetables—any of the following, alone or in combination: asparagus ends, beet tops, broccoli leaves and stems, cauliflower leaves, celery tops, mushroom stems, potato peelings, turnip tops, carrots, leeks, lima beans, parsnips, peas, snap beans, turnips
1 large or 2 small onions
1 tablesp. oil
1 to 1 ½ quarts water
1 bay leaf
1 clove
Salt and pepper, to taste
1 egg white
1 tablesp. lemon juice

1. Cut all vegetables into small pieces; chop onion.

2. Pan onion in hot oil until tender; add vegetables and brown for 5 minutes.

3. Add cold water, let come to a boil, season, cover, and simmer over a low flame for about 45 minutes. Strain through a sieve.

4. Add beaten egg white and lemon juice, cover, and let come to a quick boil; strain through a fine sieve.

CLEAR OR JELLIED CONSOMMÉ

3 to 4 cups raw vegeta-
    bles—any of the follow-
    ing, alone or in combi-
    nation: carrots, caulif-
    lower, celery, lima
    beans, peas, snap beans,
    turnips
4 to 5 small onions
1 tablesp. oil
1 to 1 ½ quarts water

1 egg white
1 tablesp. lemon juice or vin-
    egar
½ cup tomato juice
Salt, marjoram and savory, to
    taste
2 to 3 tablesps. unflavored
    gelatin or agar-agar (for
    jellied consommé)

1. Cut all vegetables into small pieces; chop onion.

2. Pan onion in hot fat until tender; add all vegetables and brown for 5 minutes.

3. Add cold water, let come to a boil, season, cover, and simmer over a low flame for about 45 minutes. Strain.

4. Add beaten egg white and lemon juice, cover, and let come to a quick boil; strain through a fine sieve.

5. Add tomato juice, season to taste, and serve.

FOR JELLIED CONSOMMÉ

Measure liquid. Use 1 tablesp. gelatin for 2 cups liquid. Dissolve gelatin in ⅓ cold liquid; heat remaining liquid to boiling, add gelatin, and stir until dissolved. Pour into mold or individual cups; chill until set. Garnish with sprigs of parsley and lemon slices, and serve.

VEGETABLE SOUPS

2 cups sliced or diced raw
    vegetables
2 to 3 tablesps. oil or butter

4 to 6 cups vegetable stock,
    or water
Salt, to taste
Chopped parsley or chives

1. Pan vegetables in hot oil for about 5 minutes, stirring occasionally to prevent scorching.

2. Cover with boiling liquid, cover, and simmer over a low flame for about 1 hour, or until vegetables are tender. Add salt after 20 minutes' cooking.

3. Serve sprinkled with parsley or chives.

This basic recipe can be varied indefinitely. The following suggestions will point the way to other combinations.

Follow preparation, and use the quantities of liquid and oil, indicated in the basic recipe, if not otherwise stated.

Carrot and Potato Soup: Dice or slice 4 to 5 carrots and 1 or 2 medium potatoes; chop 1 onion. Pan onion in oil for 2 minutes. Add carrots and pan for another 3 minutes. Add potatoes, together with liquid, and simmer until tender. Season with marjoram, paprika and a pinch of sugar.

Cucumber and Water Cress Soup: Dice or slice 1 medium cucumber (unpeeled, if skin is not bitter) and cut 1 bunch of water cress fine. Pan cucumber in fat for a few minutes. Add water cress together with liquid and simmer until tender. Season with black pepper and onion juice, stir in 1 or 2 egg yolks, let come to a quick boil, and serve.

Onion and Tomato Soup: Slice 2 to 3 medium onions into rings and cut up 3 medium tomatoes. Pan, add 3 cups of liquid and simmer for 20 minutes. Add 2 cloves and 1 small bay leaf during cooking and remove before serving.

Celery and Green Pepper Soup: Cut 4 single celery stalks into 1-inch pieces, and chop 1 medium green pepper. Pan in oil for a few minutes. Add liquid, and simmer until tender. Season with paprika and nutmeg. Serve with grated cheese in a separate bowl.

Asparagus and Mushroom Soup: Chop or slice ½ pound mushrooms; cut 5 to 8 stalks of asparagus into 1-inch pieces, leaving 2-inch tips. Pan mushrooms, add asparagus together with liquid and simmer for 30 minutes; add 2 tablesps. sherry or vermouth, if desired. Season with celery salt and savory. Serve with fried bread croutons.

If cooked asparagus is used, add to soup after it has cooked for 10 minutes and cook for another 10 minutes.

CREAMED VEGETABLE SOUPS

2 cups sliced or diced raw vegetables	Salt, to taste
2 to 3 tablesps. oil	½ cup milk and 1 egg yolk or cream (sweet or sour)
3 to 4 cups vegetable stock, or water	Chopped parsley or chives

1. Pan vegetables in hot oil for about 5 minutes, stirring occasionally to prevent scorching.

2. Cover with boiling liquid, cover, and simmer over a low flame for about 1 hour, or until vegetables are tender. Add salt after 20 minutes' cooking.

3. Stir egg yolk into milk, then stir gradually into soup; if cream is used, stir constantly while adding; let come to a quick boil once. Season.

4. Serve sprinkled with parsley or chives.

This basic recipe can be varied indefinitely. The following suggestions will point the way for other combinations.

Follow preparation, and use the quantities of liquid and oil, indicated in the basic recipe, if not otherwise stated.

Corn and Pimiento Soup: Chop 2 to 3 canned pimientos, and pan. Add 1 ½ to 2 cups drained cooked corn. Use corn liquid as part of vegetable stock. Simmer for 30 minutes. Season with paprika.

Spinach and Potato Soup: Chop 1 pound raw spinach and dice or slice 2 medium raw potatoes. Pan spinach. Add potatoes together with liquid. Simmer for 30 minutes. Season with marjoram and red pepper.

Cauliflower and Mushroom Soup: Chop ½ pound mushrooms, and break 1 small head cauliflower into flowerets (to make 2 cups). Pan mushrooms. Add cauliflower together with liquid. Simmer for 40 minutes. Season with garlic salt or onion juice.

Onion and Celery Soup: Slice 2 medium onions into rings, cut 3 single stalks of celery into 1-inch pieces, and pan. Simmer for 25 minutes. Season with black and white pepper. Serve with grated cheese in a separate bowl.

Pea and Tomato Soup: Cut up 2 to 3 medium tomatoes, and pan. Add 1 cup peas together with liquid. Simmer for 30 minutes. Season with chervil and marjoram. Before stirring in the milk, cream, or sauce, add 1 or 2 tablesps. of soup to mixture, and stir in slowly to prevent curdling.

PURÉED VEGETABLE SOUPS AND BISQUES

2 cups cooked and puréed vegetables	Salt
2 to 2 ½ cups vegetable stock, or water	Parsley sprigs or chopped chives
4 tablesps. cream or thin white sauce or butter sauce	**FOR BISQUES:**
	½ cup milk
	1 tablesp. flour
	(instead of vegetable stock)

1. Heat puréed vegetable and vegetable stock in top of double boiler. Add cream or cream sauce, beat well with rotary egg beater, and heat thoroughly. Season. If a bisque is served, use milk blended with flour instead of vegetable stock.

2. Serve garnished with parsley or chives.

This basic recipe can be varied indefinitely. The following suggestions will point the way to other combinations.

Follow preparation, and use the quantities of liquid and oil, indicated in the basic recipe, if not otherwise stated.

Cream of Pea Soup: 2 cups cooked puréed peas (fresh, canned, or dried). Season with a dash of curry or 1 tablesp. grated horseradish.

Black Bean or Lentil Soup: 2 cups cooked puréed black beans or lentils, ½ cut clove of garlic, and a few drops of Worcestershire or soy sauce. Remove garlic before serving, and add sauce after cooking is finished. Garnish with lemon slices.

Cream of Tomato Soup: 2 cups strained or puréed tomatoes, juice of 1 medium onion, 1 teasp. sugar, ½ teasp. vinegar, 1 small bay leaf. Remove bay leaf before serving. Before adding cream, add 1 or 2 tablesps. of purée to cream mixture and stir in slowly to prevent curdling.

Cream of Celery Soup: 2 cups puréed celery (preferably knob celery), 1 tablesp. tomato paste, a pinch of sugar, thyme and savory. Serve with fried bread croutons.

Cream of Pimiento Soup: 4 canned pimientos, rubbed through a coarse sieve, 1 cup thin white sauce, 6 tablesps. cream, a few drops of Worcestershire, soy or Tabasco sauce. Mix pimiento with white sauce and cream before following basic recipe. Add Worcestershire sauce after cooking is finished.

BORSCH

6 medium beets

Juice of 1 small lemon

½ to 1 tablesp. sugar

Salt

4 to 6 tablesps. sour cream

1. Shred unpeeled beets on medium shredder, cover with cold water and bring to a boil. Remove scum that forms, add lemon juice, sugar, and a little salt, cover and cook for 45 minutes or until beets are tender. Chill well.

2. Place 3 tablesps. sour cream in a bowl, add a little clear beet soup, and blend well; add additional sugar, if necessary; soup should be slightly pungent in taste, but not predominantly sweet or sour.

3. Add remaining soup and mix well.

4. Top each plate of soup with sour cream and serve.

VEGETABLE CHOWDER

3 cups diced or sliced raw vegetables: beans, carrots, cauliflower, celery, corn, parsnips, peas, peppers, potatoes and tomatoes

2 medium onions, chopped

½ cup sliced okra

4 tablesps. oil

6 to 8 cups water

Salt and pepper, to taste

1. Pan all vegetables in hot oil for 5 minutes.

2. Add water, and let come to a quick boil; cover, simmer over a low flame for about 35 minutes or until vegetables are tender, and season.

GREEN SOUP

1 pound greens, of one kind or mixed	Salt and paprika, to taste
3 tablesps. oil	1 egg yolk
1 quart water, or vegetable stock	4 tablesps. grated cheese
	Toasted bread croutons

1. Chop greens coarsely and pan in hot oil for about 5 minutes.

2. Add liquid, let come to a quick boil, cover, and simmer over a very low flame for about 20 minutes.

3. Season, and drop well-beaten egg into soup, stirring with a fork so as to form shreds.

4. Serve with a bowl each of grated cheese and bread croutons.

LEEK AND POTATO SOUP

3 to 4 medium potatoes	1 tablesp. cream, sweet or sour
3 medium leeks	
3 tablesps. butter	Chopped chervil or grated cheese, Parmesan type
4 to 5 cups water	
Salt and black pepper, to taste	

1. Peel and cube or slice potatoes.

2. Cut leeks into 2-inch pieces, and pan in hot butter for about 5 minutes, stirring frequently; add potatoes and pan for another 3 minutes.

3. Cover with boiling water, season, cover, and simmer for about 1 hour or until vegetables are tender.

4. Add cream and blend well.

5. Sprinkle with chervil or cheese, and serve.

MINESTRONE (ITALIAN VEGETABLE SOUP)

3 cups thinly sliced raw vegetables, such as cabbage, carrots, celery, chard, onion, spinach, tomatoes, romaine, snap beans, mushrooms

4 tablesps. oil

½ cup brown rice
1 clove garlic
8 to 10 cups water
Salt and black pepper, to taste
Grated cheese, preferably Parmesan type

1. Pan vegetables in hot oil for about 10 minutes.

2. Add rice, garlic and boiling water, cover, and simmer for 20 minutes.

3. Remove garlic, season and continue simmering for another 15 minutes or until vegetables and rice are tender.

4. Serve with cheese in a separate bowl.

FRENCH ONION SOUP

½ pound onions, small or large
3 tablesps. butter
5 cups vegetable stock, or water
Salt, to taste

1 small bay leaf
4 thin slices bread
4 to 5 tablesps. grated cheese, preferably Parmesan type

1. Slice onion very fine and pan in hot butter until tender and slightly brown.

2. Add vegetable stock, salt, and bay leaf, cover, and simmer for about 10 minutes over a very low flame.

3. Remove bay leaf, and simmer for an additional 15 minutes.

4. Toast bread, place in soup plates, sprinkle each slice with 1 tablesp. of cheese and pour soup over it.

5. Serve additional grated cheese in a separate bowl, if desired.

Salads

CELERY, chicory, endive, escarole, all the varieties of lettuce, peppers, radishes, scallions, young raw spinach, water cress and raw cabbage are the "classic" ingredients of the fresh green salad bowl. In spring a few leaves of the "wild greens," such as wild chicory, dandelion, lamb's quarters, mustard and sorrel, will add a special tang and should be used whenever available.

Almost all other vegetables can be used in salads, too.

It would be impossible to list all the combinations of vegetables—raw or cooked—which can be used in a salad. Here, too, personal preference, time of year, and location play a role. The following suggestions are intended merely as a help for the homemaker.

As a general rule, salad bowls will present a more attractive appearance if each vegetable is mixed with dressing separately. This allows for a varied arrangement either on individual plates or in a bowl.

Of *raw vegetables*, such combinations as the following allow for enough variety to meet everyone's taste:

> Beets, spinach, romaine, cucumber
> Cabbage, endive, tomatoes
> Red cabbage, apples, celery
> Carrots, red radishes, scallions, escarole
> Carrots, kohlrabi, tomatoes, water cress
> Celery, tomatoes, cucumber, radishes
> Peas, tomatoes, water cress, cabbage
> Spinach, tomatoes, green pepper
> Spinach, beets, water cress, radishes
> White cabbage, red radishes, chicory

The leafy greens are cut fine; tomatoes, radishes and cucumbers are sliced; pepper, celery, spinach and scallions are chopped, as well as beets, cabbage, carrots, celery knobs, and kohlrabi.

The following combinations of *cooked and raw vegetables* will be found both tasteful and easy to put together:

> Asparagus, cucumber, radishes
> Beets, green pepper, cucumber
> Celery, tomatoes, carrots
> Celery knobs, tomatoes, apples
> Peas, carrots, celery
> Corn, green pepper, tomato or water cress

ASPARAGUS SALAD

½ cup French dressing
20 stalks asparagus, cooked fresh or frozen

2 small firm tomatoes
2 hard-cooked eggs
1 teasp. prepared mustard

1. Pour dressing over asparagus and marinate in refrigerator for 1 hour; slice tomatoes thin, mix with dressing, and marinate separately for 30 minutes or more.

2. Chop eggs, and mix with mustard.

3. Arrange asparagus on platter, cover stem ends with egg mixture, and surround with ring of tomatoes.

STUFFED AVOCADOS

2 avocados
Lemon juice
1 cup cooked vegetables, alone or in combination: carrots, beets, celery

and peas
2 to 3 tablesps. French dressing
Chopped parsley or chives
1 firm tomato

1. Halve avocados lengthwise, remove pit, and sprinkle with lemon juice.

2. Mix vegetables with French dressing and fill avocado halves.

3. Chill, covered, in the refrigerator or ice box for at least 1 hour.

4. Sprinkle with parsley or chives, surround with tomato slices, and serve.

SPICY BEET SALAD

2 cups cooked diced beets	1 teasp. honey
Lemon juice	3 tablesps. chopped nut-
1 small tart apple	meats
1 tablesp. caraway seeds	2 hard-cooked eggs
1 tablesp. grated horseradish	5 to 6 black olives

1. Mix beets with lemon juice.

2. Core and shred unpeeled apple, mix well with caraway seeds, horseradish and honey.

3. Mix with beets and nutmeats.

4. Garnish with sliced eggs and sliced olives.

RAW BEET AND APPLE SALAD

2 to 3 young raw beets	1 teasp. chopped caraway
1 medium tart apple	seeds
1 tablesp. light cream	Pinch of sugar
	Lemon juice

1. Scrape beets and shred on fine shredder.

2. Core and shred apple; mix lightly with beets, cream and seasonings, and serve.

BEET AND CELERY SALAD

6 single stalks celery	4 tablesps. French dressing
1 cup cooked diced beets	Lettuce leaves

Cut celery stalks into bite size; marinate celery and beets separately in dressing for at least 30 minutes.

Shred lettuce just before serving and mix in bowl with dressing; arrange beets and celery in alternate layers or piles, and serve.

CABBAGE SALAD

1 pound cabbage, green or white
1 cup mayonnaise
½ cup chopped nutmeats
2 firm ripe tomatoes
Slivers of Swiss or Cheddar cheese
Lemon juice or vinegar, to taste

Shred blanched cabbage leaves, and mix with mayonnaise and nutmeats. Surround with alternate slices of tomatoes and cheese slivers. Sprinkle with lemon juice, and serve.

CABBAGE SALAD—VIENNESE STYLE

1 pound cabbage, green or white
3 tablesp. oil
1 tablesp. lemon juice or vinegar
1 tablesp. chopped onion,
scallion or chives
Dry mustard, red pepper, and nutmeg, to taste
2 to 3 red radishes
Caraway seeds

1. Shred cabbage fine, place in dry dish towel and beat with something heavy (rolling pin, wooden mallet, or milk bottle); this makes cabbage very tender.

2. Mix oil, lemon juice or vinegar, onion, mustard, pepper and nutmeg until well blended, and mix with cabbage.

3. Serve garnished with radishes and sprinkled with caraway seeds.

COLE SLAW

1 small white cabbage
2 carrots
1 small green pepper
½ cup mayonnaise
2 tablesps. vinegar
Salt

1. Shred cabbage on medium shredder; chop carrots and pepper fine.

2. Mix with mayonnaise, vinegar and salt, and toss lightly.

TO VARY: Use ½ cup grated pineapple or cucumber instead of green pepper.

HOT SLAW

5 tablesps. well-seasoned French dressing
3 cups shredded cabbage, green or white
1 small carrot, shredded
4 tablesps. chopped nut-meats

Heat French dressing in top of double boiler, add cabbage and carrots, and nutmeats; blend well, and heat thoroughly.

RED CABBAGE SALAD

1 pound red cabbage
4 to 6 tablesps. horseradish mayonnaise
2 tablesps. grated cheese, preferably Parmesan type

1. Shred cabbage fine, place in dry dish towel and beat with something heavy (rolling pin, wooden mallet, or milk bottle); this makes cabbage very tender.

2. Mix with dressing and toss lightly.

3. Sprinkle with grated cheese, and serve.

CARROT SALAD

8 medium young carrots
4 to 6 nutmeats
1 tablesp. sugar
4 tablesps. light cream
Lemon juice, to taste
Lettuce

Scrape and shred carrots; chop nuts. Mix lightly with sugar, cream and lemon juice.

Serve in lettuce cups.

CAULIFLOWER SALAD

1 medium head cooked   1 cup green or red mayon-
   cauliflower   naise
Lettuce leaves

Break cauliflower into flowerets, place in lettuce cups, cover with mayonnaise, and serve.

CELERY SALAD

1 medium bunch celery   Lemon juice
1 medium tart apple   Red pepper and curry, to
2 ripe bananas   taste
2 to 3 tablesps. light cream

1. Cut celery in bite size.
2. Make up dressing of grated apple, mashed bananas, cream, lemon juice and seasoning.
3. Mix with celery and serve.

STUFFED CELERY SALAD

¼ pound mushrooms   ½ cup cottage cheese
2 tablesps. oil   Lemon juice
1 large bunch celery   Salt, to taste
6 black olives   Pinch of cayenne pepper

1. Slice mushrooms fine and pan in hot oil until tender. Cool.
2. Separate celery into stalks. Chop a few inside celery leaves fine, and chop olives.
3. Mix cottage cheese with mushrooms, olives and celery leaves, and season.
4. Stuff celery stalks with mixture, and serve.

CELERY KNOB SALAD

1 medium or 2 small cooked   lic French dressing
   celery knobs   1 small pimiento, fresh or
½ cup mustard sauce or gar-   canned

1. Slice or dice cooked celery knob. Marinate in dressing for at least 30 minutes.

2. Garnish with bits of pimiento and serve.

RUSSIAN CHICORY SALAD

1 large head chicory
Russian dressing
2 hard-cooked eggs

4 to 6 black olives
Chopped dill

1. Trim off the coarse dark-green parts of chicory. Use only blanched inner parts.

2. Pour dressing over chicory and toss lightly.

3. Slice eggs in halves lengthwise, and garnish with olive halves.

4. Place on salad, and sprinkle with dill.

HUNGARIAN CUCUMBER SALAD

3 small cucumbers
2 green peppers
2 medium firm tomatoes

4 to 6 tablesps. cold garlic
sauce

1. Peel and slice cucumbers; if they are very young, they need not be peeled.

2. Cut peppers into thin strips; quarter or cube tomatoes.

3. Place all vegetables in salad bowl and mix well with dressing; chill for at least 15 minutes, and serve.

EGGPLANT CAVIAR

1 large eggplant
Lemon juice
Salt, red pepper and nutmeg,
     to taste
Chopped parsley

4 tablesps. mayonnaise
1 clove garlic
1 small head of lettuce
2 medium tomatoes

1. Wash and dry eggplant. Holding eggplant securely with a wooden fork, turn constantly over a low flame for about 15 minutes or until thoroughly black (like charcoal) and tender.

2. Place in chopping bowl, unpeeled, chop coarsely, add lemon juice and continue chopping until finely chopped. Season to taste, add parsley, and blend well with mayonnaise.

3. Crush clove of garlic and blend into eggplant.

4. Serve in nests of lettuce and garnish with sliced tomatoes.

FRENCH ENDIVE SALAD

2 small heads curly endive
French dressing
Olive oil
Mint leaves

1. Separate leaves of endive.

2. Mix French dressing with olive oil, allowing 1 tablesp. olive oil for each 4 tablesps. French dressing.

3. Mix with endive, toss lightly, and garnish with mint leaves.

KOHLRABI SALAD

3 to 4 young kohlrabi
1 tablesp. cream
1 teasp. honey
1 teasp. chopped caraway
   seeds
Chopped parsley
Lemon juice
Lettuce leaves
Red radishes

1. Peel kohlrabi only if skin is tough; shred fine.

2. Make up dressing of cream, honey, caraway seeds, parsley and lemon juice.

3. Mix kohlrabi lightly with dressing and place in lettuce cups. Garnish with radishes, and serve.

MOCK MUSHROOMS

4 hard-cooked eggs
Lettuce
French dressing
2 small firm tomatoes
1 teasp. mayonnaise

1. Peel eggs; cut a slice off one end, so that eggs will stand up.

2. Shred lettuce coarsely and mix with French dressing; cut tomatoes in half.

3. Arrange eggs on bed of lettuce, top each egg with a tomato half, and dot with well-seasoned mayonnaise.

PEA SALAD

1 cup uncooked green peas (only if very young and tender)	4 to 5 tablesps. Cumberland sauce

Mix well and chill for at least 30 minutes.

POTATO SALAD—SPANISH STYLE

6 medium cooked potatoes	1 clove garlic
4 green or black olives	¼ cup light cream
Lettuce	¼ cup tomato juice
¼ pound cheese, Cheddar type	Salt, basil, marjoram or nutmeg, to taste

1. Dice potatoes; pit and slice olives; shred lettuce coarsely; slice or dice cheese.

2. Rub clove of garlic with salt in the salad bowl in which salad is to be served. Make up dressing, in salad bowl, of cream, tomato juice and seasoning; blend well.

3. Add potatoes and mix well.

4. Surround by lettuce and top with sliced or diced cheese and olives.

SALSIFY SALAD IN TARTARE SAUCE

6 to 8 small cooked salsify roots	2 firm tomatoes or 6 red radishes
½ cup tartare sauce	

1. Cut salsify, preferably while hot, into 2- to 3-inch pieces, mix with dressing, and marinate for at least 30 minutes.

2. Garnish with sliced tomatoes or radishes, and serve.

SNAP OR WAX BEAN SALAD

1 pound cooked snap or wax
    beans
½ cup Roquefort dressing or
    sharp   mayonnaise

dressing
1 green pepper
Red pepper and onion juice

1. Cut beans into bite size.
2. Marinate in dressing for at least 30 minutes.
3. Chop green pepper fine and season with pepper and onion juice.
4. Garnish beans with green pepper and serve.

HOT GREEN SOYBEAN SALAD

2 tablesps. oil
¼ cup vinegar, heated
Salt and pepper, to taste

2 cups cooked fresh green
    soybeans

Blend oil with vinegar, and season. Mix with hot or cold soybeans, and marinate for 30 minutes before serving.

SPICY SOYBEAN SALAD

2 canned pimientos
6 green or black olives
2 cups cooked soybeans,
    fresh green or dried

½ cup sour cream mayon-
    naise
1 tablesp. grated horseradish

1. Chop pimientos; pit and chop olives.
2. Mix all ingredients, and marinate for 1 to 2 hours.

SPINACH SALAD

1 pound young spinach
1 cup Roquefort dressing

2 firm tomatoes
2 hard-cooked eggs

1. Chop cleaned raw spinach fine, put in salad bowl, and toss lightly with dressing.

2. Garnish with alternate egg and tomato slices.

STUFFED TOMATO SALAD

Chill 4 large or 8 small firm tomatoes. Cut thin slice at blossom end and scoop out pulp, leaving a firm shell. Salt inside lightly.

Fill with stuffing and top with olive or sprig of parsley.

Use pulp in soups, stews, or sauces.

STUFFINGS

Cottage Cheese Stuffing:

1 cup cottage cheese
2 tablesp. cream
2 chopped sweet pickles or
6 black or green chopped olives or

2 tablesp. grated horseradish
3 tablesps. chopped nut-meats
Salt

Mix all ingredients thoroughly.

Pea Salad Stuffing:

1 ½ cups cooked peas
½ cup mayonnaise

2 tablesps. lemon juice
Chopped parsley or chives

Mix all ingredients thoroughly.

Cole Slaw Stuffing:

1 ½ cups cole slaw

Potato Salad Stuffing:

4 cooked potatoes
3 tablesps. mayonnaise
1 tablesp. lemon juice or vinegar

Salt and white pepper
Chopped chives, parsley or dill
2 tablesps. milk

Dice potatoes, mix thoroughly with mayonnaise, lemon juice or vinegar, and seasoning and herbs. Heat milk and pour over it. Let marinate for at least 30 minutes.

VEGETABLE SALAD MOLDS OR MOUSSE

for Cooked and Raw Vegetables

2 tablesps. unflavored gelatin or agar-agar

3 cups vegetable stock, or vegetable stock and tomato juice mixed

2 hard-cooked eggs

3 cups cooked vegetables, such as asparagus, beets, carrots, cauliflower, corn, kohlrabi, peas, snap or wax beans, all diced or sliced, or

3 cups raw vegetables, such as celery, cucumber, young peas, green pepper, radishes, scallions, tomatoes, all cut or sliced

Salt and white pepper, to taste

Lettuce leaves

Chopped parsley, dill or chives

Lemon slices

1. Soak gelatin in 1 cup of cold liquid, heat rest of liquid to boiling, and add to gelatin. Stir until dissolved. Cool.

2. Line bottom of mold with slices of hard-cooked eggs.

3. Stir vegetables into dissolved gelatin, season, and pour into mold. Chill until set.

4. Unmold on bed of lettuce, and garnish with parsley, dill or chives, and lemon slices.

To make a *Mousse:* increase gelatin by 1 tablesp. and add ½ cup whipped cream before mixing with vegetables.

WALDORF SALAD

3 medium tart apples
3 tablesps. fruit juice (lemon, grapefruit, or pineapple)
3 stalks celery
½ cup mayonnaise

½ cup chopped nutmeats
Salt, red pepper and nutmeg, to taste
1 tablesp. grated horseradish
8 ripe olives
Lettuce leaves

1. Quarter and core apples, and slice crosswise; do not peel. Sprinkle with a little juice.

2. Chop celery fine, and mix with apples, mayonnaise, nutmeats and seasoning.

3. Add horseradish and mix well; chill for at least 30 minutes.

4. Serve, garnished with olives, in lettuce cups.

ICED SANDWICH LOAF SALAD

1 loaf unsliced bread
Fillings

Icing:
½ pound cottage cheese
3 tablesps. cream, sweet or sour
Salt and white pepper, to taste

Garnishing:
Lettuce
Olives
Radishes
Sliced tomatoes

1. Slice bread lengthwise into five slices and trim off crusts. Oiling the knife will make slicing easier and prevent ragged edges.

2. Spread a slice with a filling, cover with another slice, spread again, and repeat until loaf is complete.

3. Work cheese, cream and seasoning into a smooth paste, spread over top and sides of loaf with a spatula, garnish.

4. Cover with waxed paper, wrap in a damp towel, and chill for 2 hours.

5. Serve on a bed of lettuce, and garnish.

FILLINGS

½ pound cottage cheese
1 small can tomato paste
½ teasp. chopped caraway seeds
¼ teasp. red pepper or paprika
5 to 6 drops Worcestershire or soy sauce

Press cottage cheese through a sieve; mix with tomato paste, seasoning and sauce.

½ pound mushrooms
2 tablesps. oil
Salt and marjoram, to taste
Lemon juice

Chop or slice mushrooms fine, reserving a few whole to use for garnish. Blend with oil; season. Sprinkle with lemon juice.

3 hard-cooked eggs
2 tablesps. butter
1 teasp. prepared mustard
Chopped chives or parsley

Chop eggs fine and blend with creamed butter, mustard and chives or parsley.

1 well-ripened avocado
¼ teasp. each of lemon juice
and onion juice
Salt, to taste

Press peeled avocado through a sieve and mix with other ingredients.

Sauces and Salad Dressings

A SIMPLE but well made and imaginatively spiced sauce is much to be preferred to an elaborate concoction. Essentially, there are a few basic sauces with innumerable variations as to seasoning or one or another ingredient.

First and foremost is the *White Sauce*. It is used for creaming vegetables, and with slight additions or changes, can be used with fried, baked, and au gratin dishes. The thin white sauce is used in making creamed soups; the medium white sauce creams vegetables, scalloped dishes, and gravies; while the thick white sauce is best used for puddings and soufflés.

WHITE SAUCE

1 tablesp. oil
1 tablesp. flour
¼ teasp. salt

1 cup liquid, milk or vegetable stock

1. Heat oil.
2. Add flour and salt, stirring constantly until mixture begins to brown. Keep flame low.
3. Remove from flame and add cold milk gradually. Stir constantly to keep mixture smooth.
4. Place over a low flame and let come to a boil, stirring constantly. Cook for 2 minutes.

This is the so-called thin sauce. A sauce of medium thickness will result from 2 tablesps. of oil and 2 of flour, while a thick sauce can be made with 3 tablesps. each of oil and flour. In each case only 1 cup of liquid is used.

Some simple variations of this basic sauce:

Caper Sauce: Add 1 ½ to 2 tablesps. chopped capers to 1 cup medium white sauce.

Quick Cheese Sauce: Add 2 to 3 tablesps. grated cheese, preferably Cheddar type, to 1 cup white sauce, medium or thin, depending on use.

Curry Sauce: Blend 1 cup of medium white sauce with a little curry. Use curry powder sparingly, as it is very hot.

Dill Sauce: Chop dill very fine, and add to 1 cup of thin white sauce which has been blended with a little lemon juice and 4 tablesps. of sour cream or buttermilk.

Horseradish Sauce: Blend ½ cup yogurt with 1 cup of medium white sauce, add 2 to 3 tablesps. of grated horseradish, mix well; reheat if necessary.

Mock Hollandaise: Add 2 egg yolks, 2 tablesps. oil, and a few drops of lemon juice to 1 cup of medium white sauce, and blend well.

Quick Mushroom Sauce: Season 1 cup of thin white sauce with chopped parsley, red pepper and nutmeg, add ¼ pound fresh mushrooms, sliced fine and panned in a little oil, or ¾ cup canned mushrooms drained and chopped fine, and let come to a quick boil. If too thick, dilute with a little mushroom water or vegetable stock, add 1 tablesp. cream or sour cream, and simmer for 5 minutes.

Quick Mustard Sauce: Add ¼ teasp. mustard (or more if you like a hot sauce) to 1 cup of thin white sauce, and season with lemon juice and red pepper.

Tomato Sauce: Add 3 to 4 tablesps. of tomato paste to 1 cup of thin white sauce, add a few drops of onion juice, and let come to a quick boil.

Another group of sauces depends on eggs and butter either alone or together. The best-known representative of this group is the *Hollandaise,* with its two variants, Sauce Bearnaise and Sauce Mousseline.

HOLLANDAISE SAUCE

2 eggs	Chopped parsley or scallions
4 tablesps. butter	Salt and red pepper, to taste
Juice of ½ lemon	

Put all ingredients in top of double boiler and stir over boiling water until thick and creamy.

Sauce Bearnaise: Add chopped parsley, chervil, almonds and 1 tablesp. white wine or apple juice to 1 cup of Hollandaise sauce, and blend well.

Sauce Mousseline: Add 2 tablesps. of stiffly whipped cream to 1 cup of Hollandaise sauce, and blend well.

In this group belong the *Butter Sauces,* which are served hot, and their variations, such as green pepper sauce to be served hot, or the horseradish sauce which is served cold.

BUTTER SAUCE

4 tablesps. butter	pepper, to taste
4 tablesps. flour	2 cups milk or vegetable
Salt, nutmeg, basil and white	stock

1. Melt butter.
2. Add flour and stir until slightly brown.
3. Season milk and add gradually, stirring constantly.
4. Let come to a boil, cover, and cook for 2 minutes.

A thicker butter sauce can be made by using ½ cup light cream and ½ cup milk, or 1 cup milk or 1 cup vegetable stock instead of 2 cups of liquid.

Green Pepper Sauce: Add 2 finely chopped peppers to butter sauce, and let come to a quick boil.

Horseradish Sauce: Add 3 to 4 tablesps. of grated horseradish and 1 small cored and grated apple to butter sauce, and mix well.

Another group of sauces depends on *sweet or sour cream;* these can also be used as dressings. A good sauce which can be used either for hot vegetables or as a salad dressing is the simple cream dressing.

CREAM DRESSING

2 pearl onions (silver-skinned)	2 tablesps. oil
Parsley	Salt, dry mustard and red pepper, to taste
1 cup light cream	1 teasp. lemon juice

1. Chop onion and parsley very fine.
2. Blend cream with oil, add onion and parsley, and season. Mix well and chill for 20 minutes.
3. Add lemon juice and blend well just before serving.

The garlic sauce depends on cream for its character; it may be served cold with salads or hot with cooked vegetables.

COLD GARLIC SAUCE

Rub a bowl with a cut clove of garlic, add a cup of light or sour cream to the garlic in the bowl, cover, and chill for 20 minutes. Remove garlic, sprinkle with chopped parsley or chives, and use.

HOT GARLIC SAUCE

Rub a saucepan with a cut clove of garlic and a little salt. Melt 2 tablesps. of butter in the saucepan, add 1 tablesp. flour, and brown slightly, stirring constantly. Gradually add ½ cup each sour cream and vegetable stock or water, stirring constantly, and let come to a quick boil. Season to taste with salt, nutmeg, chervil and savory, and serve.

Mustard, too, makes a good variant for a cream sauce.

MUSTARD SAUCE

Mix 1 cup of sour cream with ¼ teasp. dry mustard and chopped chives or parsley, and if too thick, with a little cold vegetable stock. Blend well, chill and serve.

A good vinegar is an essential ingredient of many salad dressings. Wine vinegar can easily be made at home.

HOME-MADE VINEGAR

1 thick slice stale rye bread	1 quart water
1 quart white wine	1 tablesp. well-aged vinegar

1. Cut bread into cubes.

2. Mix all ingredients, pour into large bottle, cork tightly and allow to stand for 2 to 3 weeks.

3. Strain and pour into bottles suitable for everyday use.

NOTE: Wine that has turned sour and is no longer fit to drink is still perfectly good to be used for vinegar.

Aside from special sauces and dressings, *Salad Dressings* consist in the main of three groups: French, mayonnaise and boiled dressings. All of them can be varied in many ways by the addition of one or another ingredient. The standard French dressing is quickly made and can easily be varied.

FRENCH DRESSING

⅓ cup vinegar
½ tablesp. salt
1 teasp. prepared mustard

Dash pepper, red or black
1 cup oil

Mix vinegar, salt, mustard, and pepper well; add oil and beat until smooth.

Egg French Dressing: Chop 1 hard-cooked egg very fine and mix with dressing.

Garlic French Dressing: Rub ½ clove of garlic with salt to a smooth paste, and mix with dressing.

Roquefort Dressing: Pass 4 ounces of Roquefort-type cheese (blue or Gorgonzola) through a sieve and mix well with dressing.

Those who prefer not to use mustard or vinegar will like the following.

SIMPLE SALAD DRESSING

½ cup oil
Juice of 1 small lemon

Salt, celery salt, red pepper and basil, to taste

Mix all ingredients and chill before using.

PLAIN MAYONNAISE

1 egg yolk
1 cup oil
1 teasp. lemon juice or good

vinegar
Salt, red pepper, dry mustard, marjoram, to taste

1. Beat egg yolk with rotary egg beater.
2. Add oil drop by drop, beating constantly.
3. When mayonnaise becomes very thick, add lemon juice or vinegar a drop at a time and continue beating.
4. Season and blend well without beating.

NOTE: One egg yolk has to be used for making mayonnaise, no matter what smaller quantity is prepared.

The homemaker who does not wish to take the time to prepare mayonnaise at home will find a number of well-prepared mayonnaises on the market.

Both taste and appearance of mayonnaise can be varied easily.

Chive or Dill Mayonnaise: Blend mayonnaise with 2 to 3 tablesps. sour cream or buttermilk, chopped chives or dill, and additional lemon juice, red pepper, celery salt and marjoram.

Cottage Cheese Mayonnaise: Press ½ cup cottage cheese through sieve and blend with mayonnaise.

Green Mayonnaise: Add ¼ pound of raw spinach, which has been chopped in an electric blender. Blend with mayonnaise and add the juice of a small lemon or onion; chill before using.

Horseradish Mayonnaise: Blend mayonnaise with 2 tablesps. grated horseradish, 1 small tart apple, peeled and grated, and 4 tablesps. light cream. Chill before using.

Red Mayonnaise: Add ¼ cup red beet or tomato juice to mayonnaise. Blend well and chill before using.

Sour Cream Mayonnaise: Blend ½ cup sour cream with ½ cup mayonnaise; chill, and add 1 tablesp. lemon juice before using.

Spanish Mayonnaise: Add 1 tablesp. tomato paste, 1 finely chopped green pepper; either ½ fresh pimiento or 1 canned, finely chopped, and 6 black olives, pitted and chopped, to mayonnaise. Blend well and chill before using.

Russian Dressing: Add 1 or 2 small dill pickles, chopped fine, 4 tablesps. tomato catsup, and a few drops of soy sauce to mayonnaise. Blend well and chill before using.

BOILED DRESSING

1 tablesp. sugar
½ teasp. dry mustard
½ teasp. salt
Pinch of cayenne pepper
3 egg yolks

2 tablesps. oil
⅓ cup vinegar diluted with
   cold water to make ½
   cup

1. Mix dry ingredients, add egg yolks, and beat until thick and light-colored.

2. Add oil gradually and stir until thoroughly mixed.

3. Add diluted vinegar, place over hot water, and cook until mixture begins to thicken, stirring constantly.

Cream Dressing: Add 3 to 4 tablesps. whipped cream, and blend well.

LOW CALORIE SALAD DRESSING

1 cup buttermilk
½ teasp. dry mustard
½ teasp. salt

Red and black pepper, to
   taste
Lemon juice or vinegar, if
   desired

Mix all ingredients and chill before using.

Here are a few sauces which make an excellent accompaniment for vegetable dishes.

CHEESE SAUCE

2 cups buttermilk
2 egg yolks
1 cup grated cheese

⅛ teasp. dry mustard
Lemon juice
Salt

1. Blend milk with egg yolks, beating constantly until mixture begins to thicken.

2. Add grated cheese and blend.

3. Season and use.

CUMBERLAND SAUCE

½ cup currant jelly
½ cup cranberry sauce
3 to 4 tablesps. red wine
4 to 5 shallots or young green
    onions

Juice and peel of ¼ lemon
Juice and peel of ¼ orange
¼ teasp. dry mustard
Salt, red pepper and nutmeg,
    to taste

1. Mix all dry ingredients and stir into wine.
2. Add jellies, blend well, and add seasoning.
3. Chop onions and peelings, and add to sauce. Stir well.
4. Chill for at least 2 hours, and serve.

FINES HERBES SAUCE

1 cup buttermilk
1 teasp. each of
    chopped chervil
    chopped chives

chopped tarragon
chopped water cress
Salt and dry mustard

Mix all ingredients, season to taste, and chill for about 30 minutes before serving.

NOTE: If powdered herbs are used instead of fresh, use about half the quantity and chill for about 1 hour before serving.

MADEIRA SAUCE

½ pound fresh mushrooms
3 to 4 tablesps. butter
2 cups vegetable stock

Chopped parsley
Salt, to taste
4 tablesps. dry red wine

1. Chop mushrooms fine and pan in hot butter for 3 minutes. Stir frequently.
2. Add vegetable stock and parsley, cover, and simmer for 15 minutes, or until liquid is reduced to 1 cup. Season.
3. Add wine and simmer, uncovered, for 2 minutes.
NOTE: May be served either hot or chilled.

MUSHROOM SAUCE

½ pound fresh mushrooms or   mushroom liquid, or
   1 cup canned   half milk and half stock)
3 tablesps. butter   1 teasp. flour
Chopped parsley   Salt and red pepper, to taste
1 cup liquid (vegetable stock,   ½ cup cream

1. Slice mushrooms fine and pan in hot butter together with parsley until tender (about 8 minutes).

2. Add liquid, cover, and simmer for 5 minutes.

3. Stir flour and seasoning into cream; add to sauce, and let come to a quick boil, stirring constantly.

ONION SAUCE

½ pound onions   1 tablesp. flour
1 green pepper   1 teasp. sugar
3 tablesps. butter or oil   2 cups vegetable stock, or
Salt, paprika and basil, to   water
   taste

1. Chop onions and green pepper very fine, keeping the two separate. Pan onions in hot fat until tender. Season.

2. Add flour and sugar and mix well.

3. Add cold liquid gradually, stirring constantly. Let come to a boil, cover and simmer for 5 minutes.

4. Add pepper and simmer for another 10 minutes.

One tablesp. sugar browned in 1 tablesp. liquid can be added to sauce just before serving, if brown sauce is desired.

Index

A

Acorn squash, 32
  buying, 46
  cooking, 71
Alligator pears, *see* Avocados
Artichokes, French or globe, 32
  buying, 35
  cooking, 60
  hearts, 83
    Turkish style, 84
  Italian style, 82
  seasoning, 75
  storing, 51
  stuffed, 83
Artichokes, Jerusalem, 33
  au gratin, 84
  buying, 36
  cooking, 60
  fritters, 95
  in wine, 86
  seasoning, 75
  storing, 51
  stuffed, 85
Asparagus, 32
  buying, 36
  cooking, 23, 60
  creamed, au gratin, 87
  French fried, 88
  salad, 179
  seasoning, 75
  souffle, 86
  soup with mushrooms, 172
    seasoning, 75
  stew, 87
  with carrots, 103
Au gratin, definition, 58
Avocados,
  buying, 36
  in salads, 61, 179, 190
  in sandwich loaf, 190
  storing, 51

B

Baking, 16
  dishes, care of, 26, 27
    greasing, 26

Baking soda, avoid use of, 16
Basting, 56
Batters, 59
Beans, dried, 34
  baked, with tomatoes, 165
  Boston baked, 165
  candied, with nuts and apples, 166
  cooking, 73, 74
  soups, 174
  storing, 53
  varieties, 74
  with poached eggs, 166
  with tomatoes, 165
Beans, fava or faba, *see* Fava beans
Beans, lima, *see* Lima beans
Beans, snap, *see* Snap beans
Beans, soybeans, *see* Soybeans
Beans, string, *see* Snap beans
Beans, wax, *see* Wax beans
Bearnaise sauce, 194
Beet greens, 32, 95. *See also* Greens
Beets, 33
  au gratin, 94
  buying, 37
  cooking, 62
  custard, 93
  in Madeira sauce, 95
  salads, 180,
    seasoning, 76
  seasoning, 76
  soup, 175
  spicy, with apples, 94
  storing, 150
  with celery, 107
Bisques, 173–174
Black beans,
  soup, 174
  with poached eggs, 166
Blanching, 25, 27, 56,
Boiled dressing, 199
Boiling, 16
Borsch, 175
Boston baked beans, 165
Bread crumbs, buttering, 26
Broccoli, 32
  buying, 37

cooking, 23, 62
Italian style, 95
seasoning, 76
storing, 51
with tomatoes, 96
Broiling, 16
Brussels sprouts, 32
buying, 38
cooking, 62
without odor, 27
French fried, 97
in sour cream, 96
scalloped, 97
seasoning, 76
storing, 51
Butter,
sauce, 194
substitutes, 79
Buttermilk, in low-calorie dressing, 21

C

Cabbage, 32, 33
blanching, 26, 27, 56
buying, 38
cole slaw, 181
seasoning, 76
cooking, 62
without odor, 23, 27
creamed, Chinese, 101
goulash, 98
hot slaw, 182
in vegetable and rice casserole, 162
in vegetable stews, 162
red, fritters, 102
panned, 101
salad, 182
seasoning, 76
with apples, 102
salads, 181, 182
seasoning, 76
stew, 100
storing, 51, 52
stuffed, 99
with mustard sauce, 162
with sour cream, 98
with wine, Italian style, 100
Calcium, 4–5, 8–9, 10, 12
Calories, 4, 8–9, 10
Canned vegetables
heating, 74
storing, 52

Carbohydrates, 10, 12
Carrots, 32
au gratin, 103
buying, 38
casserole, 102
cooking, 63
glazed, with peas, 103
in cabbage stew, 100
in vegetable stews, 161, 162
minted, 104
salad, 182
seasoning, 76
seasoning, 76
soup, with potatoes, 170
storing, 51
Cauliflower, 23, 33
blanching, 26, 27, 56
buying, 38
cooking, 63
without odor, 27,
fritters, 105
in stuffed green peppers, 138
in vegetable and rice casserole, 162
Italian style, 105
salad, 183
seasoning, 76
seasoning, 76
souffle, 104
soup, with mushrooms, 173
stalks, use of, 23
storing, 51
Celeriac, see Celery knob
Celery, 27, 32, 33
braised, 106
buying, 23, 39
cooking, 63
O'Brien, 106
Russian style, 107
salads, 180, 183
seasoning, 77
stuffed, 183
seasoning, 76
soups, 172, 173, 174
storing, 51
with mustard sauce, 162
Celery knob, 33
au gratin, 107
buying, 39
cooking, 63
dumplings, 108
Italian style, 109
pilaf, 108
salad, 180, 183

seasoning, 77
storing, 51
Cellulose 5
Chard, Swiss, *see* Swiss chard
Chayotes, 33
  buying, 39
  cooking, 64
  fried, 110
  storing, 51
Cheese sauce, 199
  quick, 193
Chestnuts,
  buying, 39
  cooking, 64
  spiced, 111
Chicory, 32, 33. *See also* Endive,
    French
  cleaning, 49,
  salad, 184
  storing, 51
Chives, 25
Chopping, 26
Chowder, 175
Cole slaw, 181
  in stuffed tomatoes, 188
  seasoning, 76
Collards, 32. *See also* Greens
  buying, 39
  cleaning, 49
  cooking, 64
  Italian style, 111
  storing, 51
Condiments, 17, 75–78
Consommés, clear and jellied, 170
Corn, 32, 33
  au gratin, 112
  baked, 112
  buying, 40
  cooking, 23, 65
  deviled, 113
  fritters, 113
  in cabbage goulash, 98
  in sour cream succotash, 90
  in stuffed green peppers, 138
  soup, with pimientos, 173
  storing, 51
  with eggplant, 116
  with mushrooms, 128
  with snap beans, 91
  with squash, 153
  with Swiss chard, 109
  with tomatoes, 158
Cottage cheese,
  in nutmeat stuffing, 159

in sandwich loaf, 190
in stuffed green peppers, 138
in stuffed potatoes, 144
in stuffed tomatoes, 188
mayonnaise, 198
Cream dressing, 195
  boiled, 199
Creaming, 57
Croquettes, 59
Cucumbers, 33
  buying, 40
  cooking, 55, 65
  salad, 184
    seasoning, 77
  seasoning, 77
  soup, with watercress, 171
  stewed, 114
  storing, 51
  stuffed, 114
  with mushrooms, 129
Cumberland sauce, 200
Curly dock, 32 *See also* Greens

D

Dandelion greens, 32. *See also*
    Greens
  buying, 40
  cooking, 65
Dasheens, 33
  buying, 40
  cooking, 65
  scalloped, 115
  storing, 51
Dehydrated vegetables, 53
Des Moines squash, *see* Acorn
    squash; Squash
Dicing, 26
Dietary allowances, 8–9
  essentials, 4–6; 8–9, 10–11
Dried beans, *see* Beans, dried
Dried vegetables, *see* Legumes
Drop batter, 59

E

Eggplant, 33
  au gratin, 115
  buying, 40
  caviar, 184
  cooking, 65
  Dalmatian style, 116
  goulash, 116

salad (caviar), 184
seasoning, 77
Spanish style, 117
storing, 51
stuffed, 117
Eggs,
  in French dressing, 197
  in sandwich loaf, 190
  to increase amount of beaten egg
      whites, 23
  with asparagus, 86
  with beets, 93, 180
  with black beans, 166
  with broccoli, 94
  with Brussels sprouts, 97
  with cauliflower, 104
  with Jerusalem artichokes, 84
  with mushrooms, 126, 127
  with green peppers, 137
  with potatoes, 139, 140, 141, 142
  with sauerkraut, 149
  with spinach, 150, 151, 152
  with squash, 155
  with tomatoes (mock mush-
      rooms), 185
Endive, curly
  buying, 41
  cleaning, 49
  cooking, 65
  storing, 50
Endive, French, 33
  buying, 41
  cleaning, 49
  cooking, 66
  in Madeira sauce, 118
  salad, 185
  storing, 50
Escarole, 33
  buying, 41
  cooking, 66
  with mushrooms, 118

F

Fava beans. For recipes, *see* Fresh
    lima and soybeans
  buying, 36
  cooking, 61
Fennel, 32
  buying, 41
  cooking, 66
  seasoning, 77
  storing, 51

with rice, 119
Fines herbes, 24
  sauce, 200
Finochio, *see* Fennel
French dressing, 197
French pancake batter, 59
Fritters, 59
  cauliflower, 105
  corn, 113
  kale, 121
  parsnip, 133
  potato and spinach, 141
  red cabbage, 102
  salisify, 148
  split pea, 168
  squash, 154
Frozen vegetables,
  cooking, 74
  storing, 52
Frying, 17, 26, 58
  temperatures for deep-fat fry-
    ing, 81

G

Garlic,
  buying, 41
  French dressing, 197
  sauces, 195
Glazing, 58
Green peppers, 25, 32, 33
  broiled, 137
  buying, 44
  casserole, 136
  cooking, 68
  in cabbage goulash, 98
  in carrot casserole, 102
  in cucumber salad, 184
  in vegetable goulash, 163
  sauce, 194
  soup, with celery, 171
  storing, 51
  stuffed, 89 , 137
  with eggplant, 116
  with okra, 130
  with snap beans, 92
  with squash, 153
  with tomatoes, 159, 160
Greens, 32, 33. *See also* Spinach
  baked, 120
  buying, 41
  cleaning, 49
  cooking, 66
  omelet, 119

soup, 176
storing, 50

H

Herbs, 17, 24, 75–78
Hollandaise sauce, 194
  mock Hollandaise, 193
Horseradish, 17
  mayonnaise, 198
  sauce, 195
Hubbard squash, 32. *See also*
    Squash
  buying, 46
  cooking, 71
  custard, 155
  fritters, 154
  Russian style, 154

I

Iron, 5, 9, 11
Italian squash, *see* Zucchini

J

Jellied
  salads, 189
  soups, 170

K

Kale, 32
  baked, 120
  buying, 42
  cooking, 66
    without odor, 27
  fritters, 121
  scalloped, 122
  seasoning, 77
  storing, 51
  with tomatoes, 121
Kitchen
  equipment, 28
  hints, 23–28
Knob celery, *see* Celery knob
Kohlrabi, 33
  à la Creole, 122
  buying, 42
  cooking, 66
  fried, 123
  in sour cream, 123
  salad, 185

seasoning, 77
storing, 51

L

Lamb's quarters, 32. *See also*
    Greens
Leafy vegetables
  cleaning, 49
  cooking, 55
  storing, 50
Leeks, 39
  au gratin, 123
  baked, 124
  buying, 42
  cooking, 67
  Hungarian style, 124
  in stuffed potatoes, 144
  in vegetable stew, 161
  seasoning, 77
  soup, with potatoes, 176
  storing, 51
Left-overs,
  serving, 57
  storing, 53
Legumes, 34, 165. *See also* Beans,
    dried; Lentils; Peas, dried;
    Soybeans, dried
  cooking, 73, 74
  storing, 53
  varieties, 74

Lentils, 34
  cooking, 73, 74
  O'Brien, 167
  soup, 174
  with prunes, in sherry, 166
Lettuce, 32, 33
  baked, 125
  braised, 146
  buying, 42
  cleaning, 49
  cooking, 67
  seasoning, 77
  squabs, 125
  storing, 51
Lima beans, dried, 34. *See also*
    Beans, dried
  baked, in mustard sauce, 167
Lima beans, fresh, 33
  buying, 36
  casserole, 88
  cooking, 61
  in pepper shells, 89

in sour cream succotash, 90
O'Brien, 87
savory, 88
seasoning, 76
storing, 51
Low calorie salad dressing, 199

M

Madeira sauce, 200
Marrow, see Vegetable marrow
Mayonnaise, 197–198
Measures, 80
Menu planning, 8, 30–32. For amounts for 4 servings, see Buying Guide, 35–48, under Individual Vegetables
Minerals, 5, 9, –13
Minestrone, 177
Mock
  asparagus, 146
  caviar, 184
  Hollandaise, 193
  mushrooms, 185
  oysters, 148
  squabs, 125
Mousseline sauce, 194
Mousses, 189
Mushrooms, 33
  à la Provencale, 127
  au gratin, 126
  Bulgarian, 126
  buying, 42
  Chinese style, 127
  cooking, 67
  goulash, 128
  in batter, 129
  in cauliflower souffle, 104
  in cream, 128
  in eggplant goulash, 116
  in fennel risotto, 119
  in sandwich loaf, 190
  in stuffed artichokes, 83
  in stuffed cabbage, 99
  in stuffed cucumbers, 114
  in stuffed eggplant, 117
  in stuffed green peppers, 137, 138
  in stuffed Jerusalem artichokes, 85
  in vegetable goulash, 163
  peasant style, 129
  risotto, 129
  sauces, 193, 201,

seasoning, 77
soups, 172, 173
storing, 51
with kohlrabi, 122
with peas, 134
with potatoes 142, 144
with rice, 119, 129, 135
with squash, 153
Mustard greens, 32 See also Greens

O

Okra, 32
  au gratin, 130
  buying, 43
  cooking, 67
  storing, 51
Onions, 24, 33. See also Scallions
  baked in wine, 131
  buying, 43
  cooking, 68
  French-fried, 131
  sauce, 201
  soups, 171, 173, 177
  storing, 51, 52
  stuffed, 132
  with nuts, 131
Oven temperatures, 80
Oysterplant, see Salisify

P

Panning, 58
Parboiling, 56
Parsley, 24, 33
  buying, 43
  cleaning, 49
  storing, 50
Parsnips, 33
  buying, 43
  cooking, 68
  fried, 132
  fritters, 133
  mashed, 133
  seasoning, 77
  storing, 51
Peanuts, 34
  with parsnips, 133
  with potatoes, 144
  with Spanish onions, 131
  with tomatoes, 157

Peas, dried, 34
  au gratin, 168
  cooking, 73, 74
  fritters, 168
  storing, 52
  varieties, 74
Peas, fresh, 32
  buying, 44
  cooking, 68
  goulash, 134
  in pods, with butter sauce, 135
  in stuffed eggplant, 117
  in stuffed tomatoes, 188
  in vegetable goulash, 163
  Mexican style, 134
  salad, 186
  seasoning, 77
  soup with tomato, 173
    seasoning, 77
  storing, 51
  with glazed carrots, 103
  with mushrooms, 129
  with rice, 135
Peppers, green, *see* Green peppers
Phosophorus, 9, 11, 12
Pimientos
  in celery knob, 109
  in soybean salad, 187
  in stuffings, 138, 145, 159
  soups, 173, 174
  with dried beans, 166
  with eggplant, Spanish style, 117
  with lentils, 167
  with lima beans, 89
  with peas, 134
  with rice, 135
Potatoes, sweet, *see* Sweet potatoes
Potatoes, white, Irish, 33
  au gratin, 141
  baked, 69, 139, 143, 144
  balls, breaded, 139
  buying, 44
  cakes, fried, 139
  cooking, 69
  French-frying, 33, 69
  Hungarian style, 140
  in braised celery, 106
  in green peppers, 138
  in soybean hash, 168
  in spinach balls, 151
  in vegetable stews, 161, 162, 163
  mashing, 24
  new, 140

omelet, peasant, 140
ramekins, 142
ring, 142
salad, 186
  in stuffed tomatoes, 188
  seasoning, 78
seasoning, 78
soufflé, 143
soups, 171, 173, 176
  seasoning, 78
spinach fritters, 141
storing, 51, 52
with kale, 120
with mushrooms, 129
with mustard sauce, 162
with sauerkraut, 143, 148
Proteins, 5, 8, 10 12
Pumpkins, 32, 51, 52
Pureed—
  soups, 174–5
  vegetables, 133, 146, 155, 165
Pureeing, 58

R

Radishes, 22, 33
  buying, 44
  cooking, 69
  smothered, 145
  storing, 51
Rice
  cooking, 25
  in fennel risotto, 119
  in kale fritters, 121
  in Spanish risotto, 135
  in stuffed cucumbers, 114
  in stuffed green peppers, 137, 138
  in vegetable casserole, 162
  with celery knob, 108
  with mushrooms, 129
  with peas, 135
  with snap beans, 91
  with tomatoes, 160
Romaine
  as mock asparagus, 146
  au gratin, 145
  braised, 146
  buying, 45
  cooking, 70
  storing, 50, 51
  with celery knob, 107
Root vegetables
  cleaning, 49

...uce, 161
...vegetable goulash, 163
  peeling, 25
  seasoning, 78
  with mustard sauce, 162

V

Vegetable marrow, 33. *See also* Squash
  buying, 46
  cooking, 72
  fried, 125
Vegetable stock, *see* Stock (for soups)
Vegetables
  buying, 35–48
    amounts for 4 servings, 35–48
  casserole, with rice, 162
  chowder, 175
  cleaning, 49
  cooking, 27, 55–57
  definition of, VII
  goulash, 163
  in mustard sauce, 162
  low-calorie, VIII
  organic, IX
  quick-frozen,
    cooking, 74
    storing, 52
  serving, 57, 80
  soups, 169–177
  stew, 161
  storing, 50–53
Vinegar, 24
  home-made, 196
Vitamins, 5, 8–9, 11, 13, 14

W

Waldorf salad, 190
Water,
  amounts for cooking various vegetables 55–56
  in foods, 11
Water cress, 21, 23, 33,
  buying, 48
  cleaning, 49
  soup, with cucumber, 171
  storing, 50
Wax beans, 37, 61. *See also* Snap beans
White sauce, 192
Wild greens. *see* Greens
Winter squash, *see* Squash; Hubbard squash
Witloof chicory, *see* Endive, French

Y

Yams, 32. *See also* Sweet potatoes
  buying, 47
  cooking, 69
  seasoning, 78
  storing, 51
Yellow squash, 32. *See also* Squash
  buying, 46
  cooking, 72
  storing, 51

Z

Zucchini, 33. *See also* Squash
  a la Provencale, 163
  au gratin, 164
  buying, 46
  cooking, 72
  storing, 51

Starches, *see* Carbohydrates
Steaming, 16, 54, 55
Stock (for soups) 55, 169
  storing, 53
Storing, 50–53
Stretching tricks,
  egg whites, 24
  lemons, 24
  vegetables, 27
String beans, *see* Snap beans
Stuffings,
  cauliflower, 138
  cole slaw, 188
  corn, 138, 159
  cottage cheese, 138, 144, 188
  egg, 159
  lima bean, 159
  mushroom, 138, 144, 159
  nutmeat, 159
  olive, 145
  onion, 144
  pea, 188
  peanut, 144
  potato, 138, 188
  rice, 138, 159
  sauerkraut, 144
  soybean, 138
  spinach, 144
  vegetable, 159
    for avocado salad, 179
Succotash, 90
Sugars, *see* Carbohydrates
Summer squash, *see* Squash
Sweet potatoes 32
  baked, 69
  buying, 47
  cooking, 69
  in Cumberland sauce, 156
  in Madeira sauce, 155
  seasoning, 78
  storing, 51, 52
  with pineapple, 156
Swiss chard, 32
  buying, 39
  casserole, 109
  cleaning, 49
  cooking, 64
  scalloped, 110
  seasoning, 77
  storing, 50

  for frying, 81
  oven, 80
Tomatoes, 33
  baked, 156, 157
  broiled, 72, 157
  buying, 47
  cooking, 55, 72
  Diuvec, 159
  French fried, 157
  in cabbage goulash, 98
  in cabbage salad, 181
  in celery knob pilaf 108
  in cucumber salad, 184
  in eggplant caviar, 184
  in stuffed eggplant, 117
  in vegetable stews, 161
  peeling, 25
  salad (mock mushroom), 185
  sauce, 193
  seasoning, 78
  Serbian style, 160
  soups, 171, 173, 174
  stewed, 158
  storing, 52
  stuffed, hot, 158
    salads, 188
  with baked greens, 120
  with broccoli, 96
  with cabbage, 100
  with cheese, 156
  with chestnuts, 111
  with corn, 113
  with cucumbers, 114
  with dried beans, 165
  with eggplant, 116
  with escarole, 118
  with green peppers , 136
  with kale, 121
  with kohlrabi, 122
  with leeks, 124
  with lima beans, 88
  with mushrooms, 127, 128, 129
  with mustard sauce, 162
  with peanuts, 157
  with peas, 134
  with potatoes, 138
  with sauerkraut, 149
  with snap beans, 91
  with squash, Hungarian style, 153
  with turnips, 160
  with zucchini, 164
Turnip greens, 32, 161. *See also* Greens

T

Temperatures

seasoning, 78
steamed, Hungarian style, 149
with potatoes, 143, 144
Sautéeing, *see* Panning
Scallions, 32, 33
buying, 43
cooking, 70
custard, 130
in stuffed potatoes, 144
storing, 51
Scalloping, 58
Seasoning guide, 75–78, 79
Snap beans
buying, 37
cooking, 61
Hungarian style, 91
in vegetable goulash, 163
Italian style, 90
ragout, 91
salad, 187
seasoning, 76
storing, 51
with green peppers, 92
Sorrel, 32. *See also* Greens
Soufflé,
asparagus, 86
cauliflower, 104
potato, 143
spinach and cheese, 150
Soup(s), 169–177
asparagus and mushroom, 172
bisques, 173, 174
black bean, 174
borsch, 175
carrot and potato, 171
cauliflower and mushroom, 173
celery and green pepper, 171
consommes, 170
corn and pimiento, 173
cream of celery, 174
pea, 174
pimiento, 174
tomato, 174
creamed begetable, 172–174
cucumber and watercress, 171
green, 176
jellied, 170
leek and potato, 176
lentil, 174
Minestrone, 177
onion, 171, 173, 177
pea and tomato, 173
spinach and potato, 173
vegetable chowder, 175

Sour cream, 25
mayonnaise, 198
Soybean sprouts, 33
buying, 45
cooking, 70
in sauce mousseline, 92
storing, 51
Soybeans, dried, 34
cooking, 73, 74
hash, 168
in stuffed green peppers, 138
salad, 187
storing, 53
with kale, 122
Soybeans, fresh, 32 *See also* Lima
beans
buying, 45
casserole, 93
cooking, 61
in stuffed green peppers, 138
salads, 187
seasoning, 76
storing, 51
with kale, 122
Spices, 17, 75–78
Spinach, 32, 33
balls, 151
buying, 41
casserole, 151
cleaning, 49, 51
cooking, 71
in potato fritters, 141
in stuffed potatoes, 144
roll, 152
salad, 187
seasoning, 78
soufflé, with cheese, 150
soup, with potato, 173
storing, 50, 51
with celery knob, au gratin, 107
Split peas, *see* Peas, dried
Squash, 32, 33 *See also* Acorn
squash; Hubbard squash;
Summer squash; Vegetable
marrow; Zucchini
baked slices, 152
buying, 46
cooking, 71
French fried, 152
Hungarian style, 153
in cream, 153
panned, 153
seasoning, 78
storing, 51

cooking, 56
storing, 50
Roquefort dressing, 197
Roughage, 5, 11
Russian dressing, 198
Rutabagas, 32. *See also* Turnips
  buying, 48
  cleaning, 49
  cooking, 73
  storing, 51
  Swedish style, 146

S

Salad bowl, care of, 27
Salad dressing(s), 21, 196–199
  boiled, 199
  chive mayonnaise, 198
  cottage cheese mayonaise, 198
  cream, 195, 199
  dill mayonnaise, 198
  egg French, 197
  French, 197
  garlic French, 197
  green mayonnaise, 198
  horseradish mayonnaise, 198
  low calorie, 199
  mayonnaise, 197
  red mayonnaise, 198
  Roquefort, 197
  Russian, 198
  simple, 197
  sour cream mayonnaise, 198
  Spanish mayonnaise, 198
Salad(s), 18–22, 178–191
  asparagus, 179
  beet, 180
  beet and celery, 180
  cabbage, 181
    Viennese style, 181
  carrot, 182
  cauliflower, 183
  celery, 183
  celery knob, 183
  cole slaw, 181
  eggplant caviar, 184
  French endive, 185
  hot slaw, 182
  Hungarian cucumber, 184
  jellied, 189
  kohlrabi, 185
  mock mushrooms, 185
  molds, 189
  mousse, 189

  pea, 186
  potato—Spanish style, 186
  raw beet and apple, 180
  red cabbage, 182
  Russian chicory, 184
  salsify in tartare sauce, 186
  sandwich loaf, 190
  snap or wax bean, 187
  soybeans, 187
  spinach, 187
  stuffed avocados, 179
  stuffed tomato, 188
  stuffed celery, 183
  vegetable, cooked, 20, 179
    raw, 19–20, 178, 179
  Waldorf, 190
Salsify, 33
  au gratin, 147
  buying, 45
  cooking, 70
  Dutch style, 147
  fritters, 148
  mock oysters, 148
  salad, in tartare sauce, 186
  seasoning, 78
  storing, 51
Salt, use of with vegetables, 56, 57
Sandwich loaf salad, 190
Sauce(s), 192–196, 199–201
  Bearnaise, 194
  butter, 194
  caper, 193
  cheese, 193, 199
  cream, 195
  Cumberland, 200
  curry, 193
  dill, 193
  fines herbes, 200
  garlic, cold, 195
    hot, 195
  green pepper, 194
  Hollandaise, 194
  horseradish, 193, 195,
  Madeira, 200
  mock Hollandaise, 193
  mousseline, 194
  mushroom, 193, 201
  mustard, cold, 196
    hot, 193
  onion, 201
  white, 192
Sauerkraut, 33
  baked, 148, 149
  home-made, 149